The Floure and the Leafe

The Assembly of Ladies

The Isle of Ladies

Middle English Texts

General Editor

Russell A. Peck
University of Rochester

Advisory Board

Rita Copeland
University of Minnesota

Thomas G. Hahn
University of Rochester

Lisa Kiser
Ohio State University

Thomas H. Seiler
Western Michigan University

R. A. Shoaf
University of Florida

Bonnie Wheeler
Southern Methodist University

The Middle English Texts Series is designed for classroom use. Its goal is to make available to teachers and students texts which occupy an important place in the literary and cultural canon but which have not been readily available in student editions. The series does not include those authors such as Chaucer, Gower, Langland, the Pearl-poet, or Malory, whose English works are normally in print in good student editions. The focus is, instead, upon Middle English literature adjacent to those authors that teachers need in compiling the syllabuses they wish to teach. The editions maintain the linguistic integrity of the original work but within the parameters of modern reading conventions. The texts are printed in the modern alphabet and follow the practices of modern capitalization and punctuation. Manuscript abbreviations are expanded, and u/v and j/i spellings are regularized according to modern orthography. Hard words, difficult phrases, and unusual idioms are glossed on the page, either in the right margin or at the foot of the page. Textual notes appear at the end of the text, along with a glossary. The editions include short introductions on the history of the work, its merits and points of topical interest, and also include briefly annotated bibliographies.

The Floure and the Leafe

The Assembly of Ladies

The Isle of Ladies

Edited by

Derek Pearsall

Published for TEAMS
(Consortium for the Teaching of the Middle Ages, Inc.)

by

Medieval Institute Publications

WESTERN MICHIGAN UNIVERSITY

Kalamazoo, Michigan—1990

Library of Congress Cataloging-in-Publication Data

Flower and the leaf.
    The floure and the leafe, The assembly of ladies, The isle of
ladies / edited by Derek Pearsall.
        p. cm. -- (Middle English texts)
    In Middle English.
    Includes bibliographical references and index.
    ISBN 0-918720-43-5 : $6.95
    1. English poetry--Middle English, 1100-1500. 2. Courtly love-
-Poetry. 3. Visions--Poetry. 4. Dreams--Poetry. 5. Women--Poetry.
I. Pearsall, Derek Albert. II. Chaucer, Geoffrey, d. 1400.
III. Assembly of ladies. 1990. IV. Isle of ladies. 1990.
V. Title. VI. Series: Middle English texts (Kalamazoo, Mich.)
PR1203.F56   1990
821'.2080354--dc20   90-45121
                                                                  CIP

Fourth printing 2001

Printed in the United States of America

Cover design by Elizabeth King

Contents

The Floure and the Leafe

Introduction

The only authoritative text of *FL* is that which Thomas Speght introduced into his first edition (1598) of Chaucer's Collected Works, though there is a contemporary list of contents in the late fifteenth-century manuscript Longleat 258 (which also contains *The Assembly of Ladies*) which suggests that *FL* once occupied pages now lost in that manuscript. In including *FL*, Speght was following the practice of his sixteenth-century predecessors by enlarging his edition of Chaucer with the addition of works that could plausibly be attributed to the poet, and *FL* remained in the Chaucer canon, as one of the most admired of his poems, until expelled by Henry Bradshaw on the basis of rhyme-tests in 1868. The attribution to Chaucer is totally without historical foundation. Skeat printed a text of *FL* in the supplement to his great edition of Chaucer, *Chaucerian and Other Pieces*, in 1897, with valuable introduction and notes, and with the text restored to its presumed original near-Chaucerian form (it was actually probably written about 1460–80) by means of very extensive conjectural emendation of grammar and spelling. In this he was extremely skillful, but a modern editor, faced with a unique text of a poem at least a hundred years later than the date of composition of that poem, is less likely to engage in such wholesale reconstruction, and Pearsall, in the standard modern edition of the poem (1962), made only such changes in Speght's text as were necessary to restore sense. These changes are incorporated silently in the present text.

FL takes its origin from the real or supposed courtly cult of the Flower and the Leaf to which Chaucer refers in the Prologue to *The Legend of Good Women* and to which Deschamps had referred before him (and Charles d'Orléans after, in the English poems written in his captivity, 1415–40). Knights and ladies would declare their adherence to the Flower or the Leaf and maintain the propriety of their choice with no doubt elegant and sophisticated casuistry. The poet of *FL* gives a fresh twist to the debate by moralizing adherence to the Flower and the Leaf in terms of a contrast between perseverance and fidelity in love and fashionable fickleness and flirtation, and between honor and valor in battle and idleness.

1

This contrast is developed in the poem with a wealth of allegorical and metaphorical suggestion. The flower, which is fading and transitory, in reality as well as in some famous biblical contexts (e.g., Isaiah 40:6–8, Psalm 1:3), is contrasted with the leaf (of certain evergreen trees, especially the laurel), which is enduring; the nightingale (female), which sings of faithful and betrayed love, is contrasted with the more light-hearted goldfinch (male); the medlar, which only ripens in decay, is contrasted with the evergreen leaf and with the woodbine, symbolic of faithful attachment. The company of the Leaf engage in singing and dancing together, but only after the ladies have done their own service to the Leaf through song and dance, and the knights have jousted; the company of the Flower arrive with minstrels and proceed immediately to promiscuous singing and dancing and to worship of the daisy (where our poet either forgets or repudiates the traditional role of the daisy or *marguerite* in Chaucer and the French poets). The great storm that follows is nicely symbolic and not too unlikely in terms of English weather (an early summer hailstorm with sharp extremes of temperature): those who shelter under the laurel are protected, so to speak, by their loyalty and fidelity in love from the extremes of passion to which those more light of love are subject. The moral contrasts are unambiguous, but they are not ruthlessly pressed home: the company of the Leaf are very sympathetic to the distress of the company of the Flower after the storm, even to the extent of gathering *salades* for them to eat — not the only time the poem has the air of a modern guide to wholesome living. The ladies of the Leaf and the Flower treat each other with exquisite politeness, and the guide that the poet meets and who explains the allegory can find no worse rebuke for the followers of the Flower than that they are 'idle.'

The poem is cast in the conventional form of the allegorical love-vision, and there are many echoes of Chaucer, Lydgate, and the French poets (Guillaume de Lorris, Guillaume Machaut, Jean Froissart, and Eustache Deschamps), particularly in the elaborate seasonal and garden setting. At the same time, the poem is also in some ways highly unconventional: it is, for one thing, a 'dream-poem' in which the narrator fails to fall asleep; furthermore, the carefully contrived arbor-setting is used only as a vantage point from which the narrator has a view of events in the wide meadow beyond. In this, and in other ways, there is a sense that the boundaries of traditional allegorical love-vision are being deliberately tested. Most striking of all is the representation of the narrator as a woman: though not unprecedented, this is quite unusual, and has to do, presumably, with a tradition that women above all are concerned with the service of the Flower and the Leaf and with questions of loyalty and constancy. On the other hand, the emphasis in the explanation of the allegory is much more upon the duties of knights to fight valiantly and not to be idle than upon the opposition between constancy and fickleness in love. The exhortation seems very close to Malory's complaints about the idle habits of present-day knights or to his vivid contrast between the stable and constant love between men and women in the old days (King Arthur's days) and 'the love nowadayes, sone hote sone colde' (*Works*, ed. E. Vinaver, III.1119).

Whether the poem is actually by a woman is a question which no ingenuity, it seems, could solve, though prejudice might point a way. The poem is pervaded by an extraordinary charm and sweet reasonableness: it breathes through and softens even distressing moments and potentially severe moral judgments. It reads like a poem that Jane Bennet (of *Pride and Prejudice*) might have written. The imitation of Chaucer is intimate, though not without its awkwardness: syntax is sometimes a little less under control than one might have expected, and the versification, if all its defects are due to scribes, must have undergone an exceptionally thorough process of corruption at their hands. The rhyme royal stanza is treated in a remarkably free and un-Chaucerian manner, with little attempt to match sense to stanza-unit or to natural divisions within the stanza.

The Floure and the Leafe

When that Phebus his chaire of gold so hie	*When the Sun; chariot; high*
Had whirled up the sterry sky aloft,	*starry*
And in the Boole was entred certainly;	*Bull (Taurus)*
When shoures sweet of raine discended soft,	*showers*
5 Causing the ground, fele times and oft,	*many*
Up for to give many an wholsome aire,	
And every plaine was clothed faire	

With new greene, and maketh small flours	*flowers*
To springen here and there in field and in mede —	*meadow*
10 So very good and wholsome be the shoures	
That it renueth that was old and deede	*dead*
In winter time, and out of every seede	
Springeth the hearbe, so that every wight	*plant; creature*
Of this season wexeth glad and light.	*grows*

15 And I, so glad of the season swete,	
Was happed thus upon a certaine night:	*Happened to be in this situation*
As I lay in my bed, sleepe ful unmete	*sleep a very remote prospect*
Was unto me; but why that I ne might	*might not*
Rest, I ne wist, for there nas earthly wight,	*knew not; was not; creature*
20 As I suppose, had more hearts ease	
Then I, for I nad sicknesse nor disease.	*Than; had not; grief*

Wherefore I mervaile greatly of my selfe,	
That I so long withouten sleepe lay;	
And up I rose, three houres after twelfe,	
25 About the springing of the day,	
And on I put my geare and mine array,	
And to a pleasaunt grove I gan passe,	*did*
Long or the bright sonne up risen was;	*before*

30	In which were okes great, streight as a line, Under the which the grasse so fresh of hew	*hue*
	Was newly sprong; and an eight foot or nine Every tree well fro his fellow grew, With braunches brode, lade with leves new, That sprongen out ayen the sonne shene,	*from its* *broad; laden; leaves* *toward the bright sun*
35	Some very red and some a glad light grene;	

Which as me thought was right a plesaunt sight,
And eke the briddes song for to here *also; hear*
Would have rejoised any earthly wight. *creature*
And I, that couth not yet in no manere *could*
40 Heare the nightingale of all the yere, *throughout*
Full busily herkened with hart and with eare
If I her voice perceive coud any where. *could*

And at the last a path of litle breade *breadth*
I found, that greatly had not used be, *been*
45 For it forgrowen was with grasse and weede *overgrown*
That well unneth a wight might it se. *hardly; see*
Thought I, this path some whider goth, parde, *somewhere; by God*
And so I followed, till it me brought
To right a pleasaunt herber, well ywrought, *a very; arbor; made*

50 That benched was, and with turfes new
Freshly turved, whereof the greene gras,
So small, so thicke, so short, so fresh of hew, *hue*
That most like unto green welwet it was. *velvet*
The hegge also, that yede in compas *went around*
55 And closed in all the green herbere,
With sicamour was set and eglatere, *eglantine*

Wrethen in fere so wel and cunningly *intertwined together*
That every branch and leafe grew by mesure, *according to a set pattern*
Plain as a bord, of an height, by and by — *flat; one; in every detail*
60 I see never thing, I you ensure, *saw; assure*
So wel done; for he that tooke the cure *care*
It to make, y trow, did all his peine *I believe*
To make it passe all tho that men have seyne. *surpass; those; seen*

And shapen was this herber, roofe and all,
65 As a pretty parlour, and also
The hegge as thicke as a castel wall,
That who that list without to stond or go, *whoever; wished*
Though he would all day prien to and fro, *peer about*
He should not see if there were any wight *person*
70 Within or no; but one within well might

Perceive all tho that yeden there without *those; went*
In the field, that was on every side
Covered with corne and grasse, that, out of doubt, *without*
Though one would seeke all the world wide,
75 So rich a field coud not be espide
On no coast, as of the quantity, *region; abundance*
For of all good thing there was plenty.

And I, that all this pleasaunt sight sie, *saw*
Thought sodainly I felt so sweet an aire
80 Of the eglentere, that certainly
There is no heart, I deme, in such dispaire, *suppose*
Ne with thoughts froward and contraire [1]
So overlaid, but it should soone have bote, *relief*
If it had ones felt this savour soote. *once; sweet*

85 And as I stood and cast aside mine eie, *eye*
I was ware of the fairest medle tre *aware; medlar*
That ever yet in all my life I sie, *saw*
As ful of blosomes as it might be.
Therein a goldfinch leaping pretile *prettily*
90 Fro bough to bough, and as him list he eet, *From; it pleased him; ate*
Here and there, of buds and floures sweet. *flowers*

And to the herber side was joyning
This faire tree, of which I have you told.
And at the last the brid began to sing, *bird*
95 Whan he had eaten what he eat wold, *wanted to eat*

---

[1] *Nor with thoughts unpleasant or disagreeable*

6

So passing sweetly that, by manifold,   *by far*
It was more pleasaunt then I coud devise.   *than; describe*
And when his song was ended in this wise,   *manner*

The nightingale with so merry a note
100 Answered him that all the wood rong,   *echoed*
So sodainly that, as it were a sote,   *fool*
I stood astonied; so was I with the song   *stunned*
Thorow ravished, that, till late and long,   *Thoroughly*
I ne wist in what place I was, ne where;   *knew not*
105 And ayen, me thought, she song even by mine ere.   *again; sang*

Wherefore I waited about busily   *looked*
On every side, if I her might see;
And at the last I gan full well aspy
Where she sat in a fresh greene laurey tree,   *laurel*
110 On the further side, even right by me,
That gave so passing a delicious smell
According to the eglentere full well.

Whereof I had so inly great pleasure   *inwardly*
That as me thought I surely ravished was
115 Into Paradise, where my desire
Was for to be, and no ferther passe
As for that day, and on the sote grasse   *sweet*
I sat me downe; for, as for mine entent,   *purpose*
The birds song was more convenient,   *congenial*

120 And more pleasaunt to me, by many fold,   *by far*
Than meat or drinke, or any other thing.
Thereto the herber was so fresh and cold,   *cool*
The wholsome savours eke so comforting   *also*
That, as I demed, sith the beginning   *supposed; since*
125 Of the world was never seen or than   *before then*
So pleasant a ground of none earthly man.   *no*

And as I sat, the birds harkening thus,
Me thought that I heard voices sodainly,

	The most sweetest and most delicious	
130	That ever any wight, I trow trewly,	*creature; believe*
	Heard in their life, for the armony	*harmony*
	And sweet accord was in so good musike	*such*
	That the voice to angels most was like.	
	At the last, out of a grove even by,	*right*
135	That was right goodly and pleasant to sight,	
	I sie where there came singing lustily	*saw*
	A world of ladies; but to tell aright	
	Their great beauty, it lieth not in my might,	
	Ne their array; neverthelesse I shall	
140	Tell you a part, though I speake not of all.	
	In surcotes white of veluet wele sitting	*outer garments; fitting*
	They were clad, and the semes echone,	*each one of the seams*
	As it were a maner garnishing,	*kind of*
	Was set with emerauds, one and one,	*one after another*
145	By and by; but many a rich stone	*In order*
	Was set on the purfiles, out of dout,	*hems*
	Of colors, sleves, and traines round about,	*collars*
	As great pearles, round and orient,	*of supreme excellence*
	Diamonds fine and rubies red,	
150	And many another stone, of which I went	*lack*
	The names now; and everich on her head	*every one*
	A rich fret of gold, which, without dread,	*hair-net; doubt*
	Was full of stately rich stones set.	
	And every lady had a chapelet	*garland*
155	On her head, of leves fresh and grene,	
	So wele wrought, and so mervelously,	
	That it was a noble sight to sene.	*see*
	Some of laurer, and some ful pleasantly	*laurel*
	Had chapelets of woodbind, and sadly	*soberly*
160	Some of Agnus castus were also	*[a willow-like plant]; wore*
	Chapelets fresh. But there were many of tho	

8

	That daunced and eke song ful soberly;	*also sang*
	But all they yede in maner of compace.	*went in circular formation*
	But one there yede in mid the company	
165	Soole by her selfe, but all followed the pace	*Alone*
	That she kept, whose heavenly figured face	
	So pleasaunt was, and her wele-shape person,	
	That of beauty she past hem everichon.	*surpassed them all*

	And more richly beseene, by manyfold,	*arranged by far*
170	She was also, in every maner thing;	
	On her head, ful pleasaunt to behold,	
	A crowne of gold, rich for any king;	
	A braunch of Agnus castus eke bearing	
	In her hand; and to my sight, trewly,	
175	She lady was of the company.	

	And she began a roundell lustely,	*dance-song*
	That *Suse le foyle de vert moy* men call,	*[see note]*
	Seen & mon joly cuer en dormy.	
	And than the company answered all	*then*
180	With voice sweet entuned and so small, [1]	
	That me thought it the sweetest melody	
	That ever I heard in my life, soothly.	*truly*

	And thus they came, dauncing and singing,	
	Into the middes of the mede echone,	*meadow each one*
185	Before the herber where I was sitting,	
	And, God wot, me thought I was wel bigone,	*knows; situated*
	For than I might avise hem, one by one,	*study*
	Who fairest was, who coud best dance or sing,	
	Or who most womanly was in all thing.	

190	They had not daunced but a little throw	*while*
	When that I heard, not fer of, sodainly,	*far*
	So great a noise of thundering trumps blow	
	As though it should have departed the skie.	*split*

---

[1] *With voice sweetly modulated, delicately fine, and high-pitched*

	And after that, within a while, I sie,	*saw*
195	From the same grove where the ladies come out,	
	Of men of armes comming such a rout	*large company*

	As all the men on earth had ben assembled	*been*
	In that place, wele horsed for the nones,	*occasion*
	Stering so fast that all the earth trembled.	*Driving on*
200	But for to speake of riches and stones,	
	And men and horse, I trow, the large wones	*horses; palace-dwellings*
	Of Pretir John, ne all his tresory,	
	Might not unneth have bought the tenth party.	*hardly; part*

	Of their array who-so list heare more,	*wishes*
205	I shal rehearse, so as I can, a lite.	*little*
	Out of the grove that I spake of before	
	I sie come first, all in their clokes white,	
	A company that were for their delite	*wore*
	Chapelets fresh of okes seriall	*evergreen oaks*
210	Newly sprong, and trumpets they were all.	*trumpeters*

	On every trumpe hanging a broad banere	
	Of fine tartarium, were ful richely bete — ¹	
	Every trumpet his lords armes bere;	*trumpeter*
	About their necks, with great pearles set,	
215	Colers brode; for cost they would not lete,	*Collars; spare*
	As it would seeme, for their scochones echone	*coats of arms*
	Were set about with many a precious stone.	

	Their horse harneis was all white also.	
	And after them next, in one company,	
220	Came nine kings of armes, and no mo,	*royal heralds; more*
	In clokes of white cloth of gold, richly,	
	Chapelets of greene on their heads on hye.	*high*
	The crowns that they on their scochones bere	*bore*
	Were set with pearle, ruby, and saphere,	

---

¹ *Of delicate silk cloth (from Tartary) that was exquisitely embroidered*

10

225	And eke great diamonds many one;	*many a one*
	But all their horse harneis and other geare	
	Was in a sute according, everichone,	*matching kind*
	As ye have heard the foresaid trumpets were.	
	And by seeming they were nothing to lere —[1]	
230	And there guiding they did so manerly.	*their; properly*
	And after hem cam a great company	*them*

	Of herauds and pursevaunts eke	*junior heralds*
	Arraied in clothes of white veluet;	
	And hardily, they were no thing to seke[2]	
235	How they on hem should the harneis set;	*them*
	And every man had on a chapelet.	
	Scochones and eke horse harneis, in-dede,	*Coats of arms*
	They had in sute of hem that before hem yede.	*matching them*

	Next after hem came in armour bright,	
240	All save their heads, seemely knights nine;	
	And every claspe and naile, as to my sight,	
	Of their harneis were of red gold fine;	
	With cloth of gold and furred with ermine	
	Were the trappours of their stedes strong,	*trappings*
245	Wide and large, that to the ground did hong.	*hang*

	And every boose of bridle and paitrell[3]	
	That they had was worth, as I would wene,	*think*
	A thousand pound; and on their heads, well	
	Dressed, were crownes of laurer grene,	
250	The best made that ever I had sene.	
	And every knight had after him riding	
	Three hensh-men, on him awaiting;	*mounted squires*

	Of which ever the on on a short tronchoun	*the first; staff*
	His lords helme bare, so richly dight	*decorated*

---

[1] *And as it appeared, they had nothing to learn*

[2] *And certainly, they had no need to go and find out*

[3] *And every boss (stud) of the breast-piece of horse armor*

255 That the worst was worth the raunsoun
Of a king; the second a shield bright
Bare at his neck; the thred bare upright
A mighty spheare, ful sharpe ground and kene.   *spear; whetted; sharp*
And every child ware, of leaves grene,   *young man*

260 A fresh chapelet upon his haires bright;
And clokes white of fine veluet they were;   *wore*
Their steeds trapped and raied right   *arrayed entirely*
Without difference, as their lords were.
And after hem, on many a fresh corsere,   *charger*
265 There came of armed knights such a rout   *large company*
That they besprad the large field about.

And all they were, after their degrees,   *wore; ranks*
Chapelets new, made of laurer grene,
Some of oke, and some of other trees.
270 Some in their honds bare boughes shene,   *bright*
Some of laurer, and some of okes kene,   *noble*
Some of hauthorne, and some of woodbind,
And many mo which I had not in mind.   *more*

And so they came, their horse freshly stering   *horses; urging on*
275 With bloody sownes of their trompes loud.   *blood-curdling sounds*
There sie I many an uncouth disguising   *unfamiliar mode of dressing*
In the array of these knights proud.
And at the last, as evenly as they coud,   *in as regular a formation*
They took their places in middes of the mede,   *meadow*
280 And every knight turned his horse hede

To his fellow, and lightly laid a speare
In the rest, and so justes began   *socket for couching spear; jousts*
On every part about, here and there.
Some brake his spere, some drew down hors and man;
285 About the field astray the steeds ran;
And to behold their rule and governaunce,   *discipline; conduct*
I you ensure, it was a great pleasaunce.   *assure*

12

And so the justes last an houre and more;
But tho that crowned were in laurer grene   *those*
290   Wan the prise — their dints were so sore   *Won; prize; blows*
That there was none ayenst hem might sustene.   *against; endure*
And the justing all was left of clene,   *off entirely*
And fro their horse the nine alight anon,
And so did all the remnant everichon.

295   And forth they yede togider, twain and twain,   *together*
That to behold it was a worthy sight,
Toward the ladies on the green plain,
That song and daunced, as I said now right.   *just now*
The ladies, as soone as they goodly might,   *decorously*
300   They brake of both the song and dance,   *off*
And yede to meet hem with full glad semblance.   *looks*

And every lady tooke ful womanly
By the hond a knight, and forth they yede   *hand; went*
Unto a faire laurer that stood fast by,
305   With leves lade, the boughes of great brede;   *laden; breadth*
And to my dome there never was indede   *in my opinion*
Man that had seen halfe so faire a tre;   *Anyone*
For underneath there might it wel have be   *been*

An hundred persons at their own plesance,
310   Shadowed fro the heat of Phebus bright,
So that they should have felt no grevance
Of raine ne haile, that hem hurt might.
The savour eke rejoice would any wight
That had be sicke or melancolius,
315   It was so very good and vertuous.   *full of healing power*

And with great reverence they enclining low
To the tree, so soot and faire of hew;   *sweet*
And after that, within a little throw,   *while*
They began to sing and daunce of new;   *anew*
320   Some song of love, some plaining of untrew,   *sang; complaining; infidelity*
Environing the tree that stood upright,   *Surrounding*
And ever yede a lady and a knight.

And at the last I cast mine eie aside,
And was ware of a lusty company   *aware; vigorous company*
325   That came roming out of the field wide,
Hond in hond, a knight and a lady;
The ladies all in surcotes, that richely   *outer garments*
Purfiled were with many a rich stone;   *Ornamented at the hem*
And every knight of greene ware mantels on,   *had on (wore)*

330   Embrouded well, so as the surcotes were.   *Embroidered*
And everich had a chapelet on her hed,
Which did right well upon the shining here,   *looked; hair*
Made of goodly floures, white and red.
The knights eke, that they in hond led,
335   In sute of hem ware chapelets everichone.   *wore matching*
And before hem went minstrels many one,

As harpes, pipes, lutes, and sautry,   *psaltery (small harp)*
All in greene; and on their heads bare,   *bare*
Of divers floures, made full craftely,
340   All in a sute, goodly chapelets they ware.   *matching; wore*
And so dauncing into the mede they fare,   *go*
In mid the which they found a tuft that was
All oversprad with floures in compas.   *all around*

Whereto they enclined everichon
345   With great reverence, and that full humbly.
And at the last there began anon
A lady for to sing right womanly
A bargaret in praising the daisie;   *pastoral song in praise [of]*
For, as me thought, among her notes swete
350   She said *Si douce est la Margarete*.

Then they all answered her in fere   *in unison*
So passingly well and so pleasauntly
That it was a blisful noise to here.
But I not how, it happed sodainly,   *know not*
355   As about noone, the sonne so fervently
Waxe whote that the prety tender floures   *hot*
Had lost the beauty of her fresh coloures,   *their*

14

Forshronke with heat; the ladies eke tobrent,   *All shrivelled up; scorched*
That they ne wist where they hem might bestow.   *knew not*
360   The knights swelt, for lack of shade nie shent.   *fainted; nearly exhausted*
And after that, within a little throw,   *while*
The wind began so sturdily to blow
That down goeth all the floures everichone
So that in all the mede ther laft not one,   *was left*

365   Save suche as succoured were among the leves
Fro every storme that might hem assaile,
Growing under hegges and thicke greves.   *bushes*
And after that there came a storme of haile
And raine in feare, so that, withouten faile,   *together*
370   The ladies ne the knights nade o threed   *had not; one single*
Dry on them, so dropping was her weed.   *dripping wet; their clothing*

And whan the storm was cleane passed away,
Tho in white, that stood under the tre —   *Those*
They felt nothing of the great affray   *tempest*
375   That they in greene without had in ybe —   *been*
To them they yede for routh and pite,   *went; pity (ruth)*
Them to comfort after their great disease,   *discomfort*
So faine they were the helplesse for to ease.   *eager*

Then I was ware how one of hem in grene
380   Had on a crown, rich and well sitting,
Wherefore I demed wel she was a quene,
And tho in greene on her were awaiting.
The ladies then in white that were coming
Toward them, and the knights in fere,
385   Began to comfort hem and make hem chere.

The queen in white, that was of great beauty,
Tooke by the hond the queen that was in grene
And said, 'Suster, I have right great pity
Of your annoy, and of the troublous tene   *distress; distress*
390   Wherein ye and your company have bene
So long, alas! and if that it you please
To go with me, I shall do you the ease

In all the pleasure that I can or may.'
Whereof the tother, humbly as she might,   *other*
395   Thanked her; for in right ill array
She was with storm and heat, I you behight.   *promise*
And every lady then, anon right,   *straightaway*
That were in white, one of them took in grene
By the hond; which when the knights had sene,

400   In like wise ech of them took a knight   *each*
Clad in grene, and forth with hem they fare   *go*
To an hegge, where they, anon right,
To make their justs they would not spare   *jousts*
Boughes to hew downe and eke trees square,   *stout*
405   Wherwith they made hem stately fires great
To dry their clothes that were wringing weat.   *wet*

And after that, of hearbs that there grew,
They made, for blisters of the sonne brenning,   *burning*
Very good and wholsome ointments new,
410   Where that they yede the sick fast annointing.   *Wherever; busily*
And after that they yede about gadering
Pleasaunt salades, which they made hem eat   *salad herbs*
For to refresh their great unkindly heat.

The lady of the Leafe then began to pray
415   Her of the Floure (for to my seeming   *it seems to me*
They should be, as by their array)
To soupe with her, and eke, for any thing,   *dine; by all means*
That she should with her all her people bring.
And she ayen, in right goodly manere,
420   Thanketh her of her most friendly cheare,

Saying plainly that she would obay
With all her hart all her commaundement.
And then anon, without lenger delay,   *longer*
The lady of the Leafe hath one ysent   *sent*
425   For a palfray, after her intent,   *palfrey; in pursuance of*
Araied well and faire in harneis of gold,
For nothing lacked that to him long should.   *belong*

16

And after that, to all her company
She made to purvey horse and every thing
430 That they needed; and then, full lustily,
Even by the herber where I was sitting,
They passed all, so pleasantly singing
That it would have comforted any wight.
But then I sie a passing wonder sight: *wondrous*

435 For then the nightingale, that all the day
Had in the laurer sete and did her might   *sat*
The whol service to sing longing to May,   *belonging*
All sodainly gan to take her flight,
And to the lady of the Leafe forthright
440 She flew, and set her on her hond softly,
Which was a thing I marveled of greatly.

The goldfinch eke, that fro the medill tre   *medlar*
Was fled for heat into the bushes cold,   *cool*
Unto the lady of the Flower gan fle,   *fly*
445 And on hir hond he set him, as he wold,
And pleasantly his wings gan to fold;
And for to sing they pained hem both as sore
As they had do of all the day before.   *done*

And so these ladies rode forth a great pace,
450 And all the rout of knights eke in fere.
And I, that had sene all this wonder case,   *incident*
Thought I would assay, in some manere,   *try*
To know fully the trouth of this matere,
And what they were that rode so pleasantly.
455 And when they were the herber passed by

I drest me forth, and happed to mete anon   *stepped; happened*
Right a faire lady, I you ensure;   *A very*
And she come riding by hir selfe alone,   *came*
All in white, with semblance ful demure.   *looks*
460 I saluted her, and bad her good aventure   *greeted; fortune*
Must her befall, as I coud most humbly,   *Might*
And she answered, 'My doughter, gramercy.'   *many thanks*

17

'Madam,' quod I, 'if that I durst enquere   *enquire*
Of you, I would faine, of that company,   *gladly*
465   Wit what they be that past by this arbere?'   *Know*
And she ayen answered right friendly:
'My faire doughter, all tho that passed hereby
In white clothing, be servants everichone
Unto the Leafe, and I my selfe am one.

470   Se ye not her that crowned is,' quod she,
'All in white?' 'Madame,' quod I, 'yis.'   *yes*
'That is Diane, goddes of chastity;
And for bicause that she a maiden is,
In her hond the braunch she bereth, this
475   That Agnus castus men call properly.   *(see note l. 160)*
And all the ladies in her company

Which ye se of that hearb chaplets weare
Be such as han kepte alway her maidenhede.   *have*
And all they that of laurer chaplets beare
480   Be such as hardy were and wan by deed   *won*
Victorious name which never may be dede;   *dead*
And all they were so worthy of ther hond,
In hir time, that none might hem withstond.   *their*

And tho that weare chapelets on ther hede   *head*
485   Of fresh woodbind, be such as never were
To love untrue in word, thought, ne dede,   *deed*
But aye stedfast; ne for pleasance, ne fere,   *fear*
Thogh that they shuld their harts all to-tere, *tear to pieces*
Would never flit, but ever were stedfast,   *waver*
490   Till that their lives there asunder brast.'   *burst*

'Now, faire madame,' quod I, 'yet I would pray
Your ladiship, if that it might be,
That I might know, by some maner way —
Sith that it hath liked your beaute   *pleased*
495   The trouth of these ladies for to tell me —
What that these knights be, in rich armour,
And what tho be in grene, and weare the flour,

And why that some did reverence to the tre
And some unto the plot of floures faire?'
500 'With right good will, my fair doghter,' quod she,
'Sith youre desire is good and debonaire.   *courteous*
Tho nine crowned be very exemplaire   *model*
Of all honour longing to chivalry,   *appertaining*
And those, certaine, be called the Nine Worthy,

505 Which ye may se riding all before,
That in her time did many a noble dede,   *their*
And for their worthines ful oft have bore
The crowne of laurer leaves on their hede,
As ye may in your old bookes rede;
510 And how that he that was a conquerour
Had by laurer alway his most honour.

And tho that beare bowes in their hond   *boughs*
Of the precious laurer so notable,
Be such as were, I woll ye understond,   *want (to)*
515 Noble knights of the Round Table,
And eke the Douseperis honourable;
Which they beare in signe of victory —   *That which*
It is witnes of their dedes mightily.

Eke there be knights old of the Garter,
520 That in her time did right worthily;
And the honour they did to the laurer
Is for thereby they have their laud wholly,   *praise*
Their triumph eke and marshall glory;   *martial*
Which unto them is more parfit riches   *perfect*
525 Then any wight imagine can or gesse.   *Than*

For one leafe given of that noble tre
To any wight that hath done worthily,
And it be done so as it ought to be,   *If*
Is more honour then any thing earthly.
530 Witnes of Rome that founder was, truly,   *[him] of Rome*
Of all knighthood and deeds marvelous —
Record I take of Titus Livius.

And as for her that crowned is in greene,   *her in green that is crowned*
It is Flora, of these floures goddesse.
535   And all that here on her awaiting beene,
It are such that loved idlenes
And not delite of no busines
But for to hunt and hauke, and pley in medes,
And many other such idle dedes.

540   And for the great delite and pleasaunce
They have to the floure, and so reverently
They unto it do such obeisaunce,
As ye may se.' 'Now, faire madame,' quod I,
'If I durst aske what is the cause and why
545   That knights have the signe of honour
Rather by the leafe than by the floure?'

'Sothly, doughter,' quod shee, 'this is the trouth: *Truly*
For knights ever should be persevering
To seeke honour without feintise or slouth,   *deceit*
550   Fro wele to better, in all maner thing;
In signe of which, with leaves aye lasting
They be rewarded after their degree,   *according to their rank*
Whose lusty green May may not appaired be,   *vigorous; impaired*

But aye keping their beauty fresh and greene,
555   For there nis storme that may hem deface,   *is not*
Haile nor snow, wind nor frosts kene;
Wherfore they have this propertie and grace.
And for the floure within a little space
Woll be lost, so simple of nature
560   They be, that they no greevance may endure,

And every storme will blow them soone away,
Ne they last not but for a season —
That is the cause, the very trouth to say,
That they may not, by no way of reason,
565   Be put to no such occupacion.'   *function (use)*
'Madame,' quod I, 'with all mine whole servise
I thanke you now, in my most humble wise;

	For now I am acertained throughly	*apprised*
	Of every thing I desired to know.'	
570	'I am right glad that I have said, sothly,	*truly*
	Ought to your pleasure, if ye will me trow,'	*believe*
	Quod she ayen, 'but to whome doe ye owe	
	Your service? and which woll ye honour,	
	Tell me, I pray, this yeere, the Leafe or the Flour?'	
575	'Madame,' quod I, 'though I least worthy,	
	Unto the Leafe I owe mine observaunce.'	
	'That is,' quod she, 'right well done, certainly,	
	And I pray God to honour you avaunce,	*advance you to honor*
	And kepe you fro the wicked remembraunce	
580	Of Male Bouch, and all his crueltie;	*Slander*
	And all that good and well-condicioned be.	*And [so with]; of good disposition*
	For here may I no lenger now abide;	
	I must follow the great company	
	That ye may see yonder before you ride.'	
585	And forth, as I couth, most humbly,	*forthwith*
	I tooke my leve of her as she gan hie	*hasten*
	After them, as fast as ever she might.	
	And I drow homeward, for it was nigh night,	*drew*
	And put all that I had seen in writing,	
590	Under support of them that lust it to rede.	*In the hope of support; desire*
	O little booke, thou art so unconning,	*ignorant*
	How darst thou put thy self in prees for drede?	*[the] throng*
	It is wonder that thou wexest not rede,	*red*
	Sith that thou wost ful lite who shall behold	*knowest*
595	Thy rude language, full boistously unfold.	*rough; set forth in homely*
		fashion

EXPLICIT

Notes

1–14   The spring opening was conventional in courtly love-allegory, as a way of suggesting the renewal of love and love's expectation, or the unhappiness by contrast of unrequited love (both suggestions are explicitly denied here, in lines 18–21).

1–3   Astronomical allusion as a way of indicating the season was equally conventional. The opening lines of the General Prologue to the *Canterbury Tales* are the best-known example. These lines are directly imitated from the closing lines of The Squire's Tale ('Apollo whirleth up his chaar so hye', V.671). Readers of poems like *FL* would be familiar from the Calendars in their Books of Hours with pictures of Phoebus passing across a starry sky in his golden chariot; the reference of course is not to the rising of the sun but to its northward course through the zodiac and its entry into Taurus (on April 12, in Chaucer's time).

8   *maketh*: It is difficult to find a subject for this verb, but loose and diffused syntax of this kind is not uncommon among those who tried to imitate Chaucer's consummate mastery of the long verse sentence (e.g., General Prologue, 1–18).

18–21   The narrator seems aware of the usual cause of sleeplessness, in love-longing and love-sickness, as in Chaucer's *The Book of the Duchess*.

27–126   The description of the garden is full of echoes of Chaucer, Lydgate, and the French poets. Like the Prologue to the *The Legend of Good Women*, it is meant to be recognized as a tapestry of literary allusion (rather than a description of a 'real' garden).

34   The sun seems to have risen very suddenly (cf. 28); consistency of realistic visualization is not in general much sought after in these descriptions.

35   *Some very red*: this, on the other hand, is a piece of precisely observed botanical detail.

40   *nightingale*: it was thought a good omen, foretelling success in love, to hear the nightingale before the cuckoo upon the advent of both with spring.

49   *herber*: The enclosed arbor was a favorite feature of medieval gardens, real and literary; lovers discourse there privately, and poets fall asleep. This poet, for a change, does not fall asleep, and the arbor exists as a vantage-point from which to view operations *outside*.

50   *benched*: earthen benches topped with turf were very popular in medieval gardens (as in the Prologue to the *The Legend of Good Women*).

78–84   The sweet scents of gardens are much emphásized; they were not only pleasant in themselves, but were believed to have healing power.

86   *medle:* The medlar tree is stunted and has low-hanging branches; the fruit is small, hard and round, and fit to eat only when decaying, when it turns brown (its popular name was 'open-ers'; see Chaucer, The Reeve's Tale, I.3871).

141   *surcotes*: sleeveless over-garments, often richly embroidered and decorated, worn over a lighter under-garment. In the fifteenth century the arm-openings became so exaggeratedly large that the top became almost like a pinafore.

142   *semes*: In the richest clothes, ornamental strips of material, sometimes studded with precious stones, were inserted or laid over the seams.

160   *Agnus castus*: a willow-like plant, emblematic of chastity.

176   *roundell*: a dance-song, led by a soloist, at the head of a chain or in the middle of a circle (as here), the soloist singing the verses of the song and the chorus repeating part of the verse as a refrain.

177–78   Popular songs were often quoted in courtly poems to give an air of freshness and topicality. The lines quoted here are a garbled version of the opening of a fifteenth-century song from Normandy: 'Dessoubz la branche d'ung verd moy, / S'est mon jolli cueur endormy' (Beneath the branch of a green May-tree / My joyful heart has gone to sleep). It is the song of a woman, describing how she is waiting for her lover, and affirming the constancy of her love.

202   *Pretir John*: Prester John, the fabulously wealthy legendary Christian monarch ('Prester' is from the same root as 'priest'), first associated with Asia, later with Ethiopia.

209   *okes seriall*: directly imitated from The Knight's Tale, I.2290, where Emelye wears a 'coroune of a grene ook cerial' as an emblem of her service to Diana. The association intended is clearly with the evergreen or holm-oak (*ilex*), though the original reference in Boccaccio's *Teseide* (which Chaucer follows), is to the deciduous Turkey oak.

220   *kings of armes*: heralds in royal employ. Here, there is one in attendance on each of the Nine Worthy (see 240).

233   *veluet*: trisyllabic here, as in Chaucer.

271   *kene*: 'noble, brave'; by hypallage, the epithet appropriate to those who bear the oak is transferred to the oak itself.

285   *steeds*: i.e., the riderless horses.

316   *enclining*: One expects a finite verb, but this rather loose use of participles is common in fifteenth-century poetry (cf. 320 below; 8 above).

329   *greene*: The symbolism of white (for purity), worn by the company of the leaf, was clear enough; green was commonly associated with, among other things, fickleness in love and frivolity, as in Chaucer's poem *Against Women Unconstant* ('In stede of blew, thus may ye were al grene').

331–33 These lines refer to the women in the company.

348   *bargaret*: from French *bergerette*, a shepherd's song, which gave its name to a fixed-form court-song in the fifteenth century. The praise of the daisy is a

convention in the French poetry of the fourteenth century and in Chaucer's Prologue to his *The Legend of Good Women.*

350 *Si douce,* etc.: 'So sweet is the daisy.' Probably the refrain of a popular song (cf. 177–78).

356 *whote*: a spelling indicative of the development of a strong rounded on-glide before *ho* (with long vowel), as in *whole, whore,* where the spelling survives.

403 *to make their justs*: It sounds as if they plan to joust with them afterwards, but this seems unlikely. The line may be corrupt.

407 *hearbs*: The botanical part of the natural history in the Middle Ages was largely the study of the medicinal properties of plants. Everyone would have known what plants to gather to make a sunburn lotion.

412 *salades*: Parsley and lettuce, specifically, are recommended for those who are over-heated (lettuce, incidentally, was also thought to be an antiaphrodisiac).

425 *palfray*: A palfrey would be a saddle-horse for ordinary riding, especially suitable for ladies.

437 *service*: The idea that the song of the birds in spring was a 'service' in honor of God, or Nature, or Love, was a popular conceit with medieval poets, characteristic of the way religious language was appropriated to the celebration of love.

456 *happed*: Such 'chance' meetings are common in allegorical poetry, where some kind of fictional guide is needed to explain the significance of what has been happening.

471 *yis*: 'yes'; was originally, as here, the emphatic form of *ye* or *yea*, and used to answer questions in a negative form.

504 The *Nine Worthy* (properly so, not 'the Nine Worthies') appear frequently in late medieval literature and art as types of nobility, illustrious examples for

the present, and, in the *Ubi sunt* ('Where are ... ?') topos, as examples of the power of death. They were, traditionally, three Jews (Joshua, David, Judas Maccabeus), three pagans (Hector, Alexander, Julius Caesar), and three Christians (Arthur, Charlemagne, Godfrey of Boulogne). Their presence here may seem odd, but the Middle Ages had little difficulty in imaging forth the past in terms of idealized contemporary chivalry. Julius Caesar, indeed, is seen as the founder of medieval chivalry (see 530–32 below).

516   *Douseperis*: *Les douze pers*, the twelve peers of France, were Charlemagne's paladins (Roland, Oliver, etc.), who fought with him against the Saracens.

519   *Garter*: The Order of the Garter was established by Edward III in 1349.

530   The reference is to Julius Caesar, who was much venerated in the Middle Ages, and credited with the founding of chivalry.

532   *Titus Livius*: Livy (59 BC – AD 17) is not renowned as a historian of Caesar, but he is an unimpeachable historical authority, which is the reason he is alluded to here.

536   *idlenes*: for moralists, the 'mother of all vices'; she is also, it is worth remembering, the portress of the Garden of Love in the *Roman de la Rose*.

541   *and*: this word upsets the grammar of the sentence, to modern taste, but such sentences are not uncommon in fifteenth-century poetry.

550   *For wele to better*: an echo, perhaps, of the idiom of the French motto, *De bien en mieulx*. Cf. *De mieulx en mieulx*, used as a motto in the fifteenth century by the Paston family of Norfolk.

554   *keping*: another loosely related participle.

565   *no such occupacion*: i.e., no such occupation (function) as to symbolize perseverance and fidelity.

574   *this yeere*: refers to *honour*, of course, not *tell*. In the courtly cult of the Flower and the Leaf, the choice was made on the first of May and was binding for the ensuing year.

580   *Male Bouch*: 'Wicked Tongue,' or Slander, a personification in the *Roman de la Rose* (called 'Wykked-Tonge' in Chaucer's translation, 3027).

591–95 A good example of the 'modesty epilogue,' which Lydgate, in particular, develops in an immodestly elaborate way. The 'little book' is probably an echo of Chaucer's *Troilus* V.1786. The characterization of the little book as blushing at its own boldness is an unusual and effective touch.

The Assembly of Ladies

Introduction

There are three manuscripts of *The Assembly of Ladies* (*AL*), all dating from the last quarter of the fifteenth century: British Library MS Addit.34360, Trinity College, Cambridge, MS R.3.19, and Longleat House MS 258. The earliest and best of these, copied not long after the poem was written (c. 1470–80), is MS Addit.34360, which is used as the basis of the standard modern edition of the poem (Pearsall 1962). Pearsall's text is followed here, with his emendations silently incorporated. There is also an early print of the poem in the collected edition of Chaucer's Works put together by William Thynne in 1532. Thynne's text, which is close to that of the Longleat MS, was used by Skeat as the basis for his edition of *AL* in *Chaucerian and Other Pieces* (1897), but solely for reasons of convenience: it has no authority. Thynne included the poem because of his desire to include all plausibly Chaucerian pieces that he could find, and it stayed in the canon until rejected by Thomas Tyrwhitt in his 'Account of the Works of Chaucer' in his great edition of the *Canterbury Tales* (1775–78). *AL* came to be closely associated with *FL* (which was also once in Longleat 258) because Skeat supposed that, since both had a female narrator, both must be by women, and, for economy's sake, by the same woman. Whatever the grounds for the attribution of the two poems to women, there are no grounds whatsoever for the attribution of both to the same author: the briefest acquaintance with the two poems will make clear the difference between the radiant and eccentric gifts of the author of *FL* and the skillful hack-work of *AL*. Style, language, and meter are all against common authorship.

The theme of *AL* is the truth and loyalty of women and, generally speaking, the neglect and unfaithfulness of men. It describes an assembly at which a group of five ladies (including the narrator) and four gentlewomen present their written complaints against men at the court of Lady Loyalty and seek redress (though exactly what form that might take remains a mystery). One of the gentlewomen seems to be there under false pretenses, since her petition (673–79) says she has nothing to complain about. The preparations for attending the assembly, the arrangements when the ladies arrive, and the organization of their presentation of their 'bills,' occupy the greater part of the poem.

The theme of the poem is a conventional one in the love poetry of the period, and bears the same relation to reality as the opposed theme of women's lasciviousness and fickleness. The paintings of women unfortunate in love in Lady Loyalty's palace (456–66) remind us of similar paintings in the temples of the *The Parliament of Fowls* and Lydgate's *Temple of Glass*, but more especially of the stories of faithful women wronged by men in Chaucer's martyrology of Cupid's saints, *The Legend of Good Women*. Chaucer represents himself, not entirely seriously, as doing penance for having slandered women in *Troilus and Criseyde*; the writings of Christine de Pisan are a good deal less playful, and her *Epistre au Dieu d'Amours* is a vehement defence of the honor and fidelity of women, particularly against the slanders of Ovid and of Jean de Meun in the *Roman de la Rose*. The debate, with its own painful basis in reality and yet no doubt productive of much lively casuistry on relaxed social occasions, continued through the fifteenth century in the controversy provoked or supposedly provoked by Alain Chartier's portrayal of the cruel mistress in *La Belle Dame sans Merci*. At the same time, it should be remembered that the theme of women wronged, oppressed, or unfortunate in love produces some of the most affecting poetry of the period, not only in Chaucer, but also, and perhaps more notably, in Gower.

The framework chosen for the development of the theme is that of the Court of Love, conceived of here both as the quasi-religious court of Lady Loyalty, where she hears petitions and grants boons, and as a court of law, with set procedure and forms of legal redress (see 325n). There are many precedents for both conventions, particularly in poems of the fifteenth century such as Lydgate's *Temple of Glass*, which is an important influence throughout *AL*; one recalls too the establishment of a *Cour Amoureuse* by the Duke of Burgundy on St. Valentine's Day, 1401, dedicated to the virtues of humility and fidelity and to the service of ladies, in whom those virtues are so conspicuous. The *complaintes d'amour* for which such assemblies provided the occasion are themselves a favorite literary genre, exploited, it must be said, more than fully in *AL*. The allegory of the assembly is enclosed within the conventional framework of a dream, which springs naturally from the circumstances of the narrator: unhappy in love, she dreams of the court of Lady Loyalty, where the wrongs of despised lovers will be set right.

The allegory of *AL* has little vitality, and it was an error of judgment on the poet's part to suppose that interest could be sustained through nine separate and generally similar petitions of complaint summarily presented (582–707). If the ladies and their mottoes were once excitingly identifiable in real life and had some topical significance in the 'game of love' (for which see Stevens, *Music and Poetry*), things might be different, but, whatever that significance might have been, it is now lost. The author's principal interest, as C. S. Lewis discerned, appears to be in 'the stir and bustle of an actual court, the whispered conversations, the putting on of clothes, and the important comings and goings' (*Allegory of Love*, p. 250). Here, in a manner reminiscent of Skelton, the dialogue has a vivid colloquial vigor, and the narrator's pert self-confidence comes over quite sharply, as in the somewhat petulant response to the request for her bill (682, 690), and in the skillfully circumspect and maybe unnecessarily suspicious way she deals with the request by Perseveraunce for privileged advance information about the ladies' mottoes (400–13). The interest in the actual running of a great household, and what may seem to a modern reader an inordinate care to name and specify the functions of all the officers, show, and are designed to show, a fair expertise; it was an interest shared by the scribes of the Longleat and Trinity manuscripts, who both rubricate appropriate stanza headings with the names of officers. In its concern for the topical and actual, *AL* stands in sharp contrast to *FL*, reflecting contemporary social life and the appurtenances of that life with a directness absent from the latter poem. There may be some specific influence from the Burgundian styles made fashionable during the later reign of Edward IV (1471–83).

Whether the author was indeed a woman is a question impossible to prove either way. There is nothing very unusual in the writing of poetry by women in the fifteenth century, nor in the adoption of a female persona by male poets. The carefully guarded language in which the exclusion of men from the assembly is first announced (145–54) suggests a certain sensitivity on the matter, as does the almost total absence (though see 669) of any mention, in the actual complaints, of men or of the fact that men are the cause of all the trouble. The language, in fact, is so vague and unspecific that one could not be sure exactly what the ladies are complaining about if one did not already know. The constant references to clothes, and the putting on and wearing of clothes, and the comments on the way the clothes look (e.g., 256), suggests a woman's interests, though they may equally well be what a man would characterize as a woman's interests. But the monotonously regular nature of the versification, the rather threadbare repertoire of tags and conventional phrases, suggest a hack versifier, and if this versifier is also responsible for the romance of *Generydes*, as seems to me certain, it is very unlikely that it is a woman. Women had occasion and good reason to write in the fifteenth century, but not like this.

The Assembly of Ladies

In Septembre, at fallyng of the leef,
The fressh season was al to-gydre done — *altogether*
And of the corn was gadred in the sheef; — *gathered*
In a gardyn, abowte tweyne after none, — *two in the afternoon*
5   There were ladyes walkyng, as was ther wone, — *custom*
Foure in nombre, as to my mynde doth falle, — *come*
And I the fift, symplest of alle.

Of gentil wymmen foure ther were also,
Disportyng hem everiche after theyr guyse, — *themselves each; fashion*
10   In crosse aleys walkyng be two and two,
And som alone after theyr fantasyes. — *according to their fancies*
Thus occupied we were in dyvers wise, — *various ways*
And yit in trowth we were nat alone: — *yet*
Theyr were knyghtis and squyers many one. — *many a one*

15   Whereof I serve? on of hem asked me. — *What am I doing here?*
I seyde ageyne, as it fil in my thought: — *in reply; came*
'To walke aboute the mase, in certeynte, — *maze*
As a womman that nothyng rought.' — *had no cares*
He asked me ageyn whom I sought
20   And of my coloure why I was so pale.
'Forsoth,' quod I, 'and therby lith a tale.' — *said; lies*

'That must me wite,' quod he, 'and that anon; — *I know; straightway*
Telle on, late se, and make no taryeng.' — *let me see; delay*
'Abide,' quod I, 'ye be an hasti one;
25   I let yow wite it is no litle thyng; — *know*
But for because ye have a grete longyng
In yowre desire this procese for to here — *hear*
I shal yow telle the playne of this matiere. — *full truth*

32

It happed thus that in an afternone   *happened*

30 My felawship and I, bi one assent,

Whan al oure other busynesse was done,

To passe oure tyme in to this mase we went   *maze*

And toke oure weyes yche aftyr other entent:[1]

Som went inward and went they had gon oute,   *and thought*

35 Som stode amyddis and loked al aboute;   *in the middle*

And soth to sey som were ful fer behynde   *to tell the truth; far*

And right anon as ferforth as the best;   *far forward*

Other there were, so mased in theyr mynde,   *bewildered*

Al weys were goode for hem, both est and west.   *ways; them*

40 Thus went they furth and had but litel rest,

And som theyr corage dide theym so assaile   *impetuous spirit*

For verray wrath they stept over the rayle.

And as they sought hem self thus to and fro[2]

I gate my self a litel avauntage;   *got*

45 Al for-weryed, I myght no further go,   *completely exhausted*

Though I had wonne right grete for my viage;   *greatly; journey*

So come I forth into a streyte passage,   *came; narrow*

Whiche brought me to an herber feyre and grene   *arbor fair*

Made with benchis ful craftily and clene;   *skillfully; neatly*

50 That, as me thought, myght no creature

Devise a bettir by proporcioun.   *a better proportioned one*

Save it was closed wele, I yow ensure,   *Safely; assure*

With masonry of compas environ   *in a circle all around*

Ful secretly, with steyres goyng down

55 In myddes the place, a tornyng whele, sertayne,

And upon that a pot of margoleyne;   *marjoram*

With margarites growyng in ordynaunce   *daisies; in regular patterns*

To shewe hem self as folk went to and fro,

That to behold it was a grete plesaunce;

---

[1] *And took our ways, each according to a different plan*

[2] *And as they looked out to and fro for an advantage for themselves*

60 And how they were accompanyed with mo,   *others*
    Ne m'oublie-mies and sovenez also; [1]
    The poore penses ne were nat disloged there —   *pansies; excluded*
    No, no, God wote, theyr place was every where.   *knows*

    The floore beneth was paved faire and smoth
65 With stones square of many dyvers hewe
    So wele joyned that, for to sey the soth,
    Al semed on, who that non other knewe.   *a single unbroken whole*
    And underneth the streames, newe and newe,   *springs; ever afresh*
    As silver newe bright spryngyng in such wise   *fashion*
70 That whens it com ye cowde it nat devise.   *whence; came; could*

    A litel while thus was I alone
    Beholdyng wele this delectable place;
    My felawshyp were comyng everichone   *each one*
    So must me nede abide as for a space,   *So I had of necessity to; time*
75 Remembryng of many dyvers cace   *happenings*
    Of tyme past, musyng with sighes depe,
    I set me downe and there fil in slepe.   *fell*

    And as I slept me thought ther com to me
    A gentil womman metely of stature;   *moderate*
80 Of grete worship she semed for to be,   *honor and worthiness*
    Atired wele, nat hye but bi mesure,   *grandly; soberly*
    Hir contenaunce ful sad and ful demure,   *grave*
    Hir colours blewe, al that she had upon;
    Theyr com no mo but hir silf alon.   *There; others; herself*

85 Hir gowne was wele enbrowdid, certaynly,   *embroidered*
    With sovenez aftir hir owne devise;   *remember-me's; emblem*
    On the purfil hir word, by and by,   *hem; motto; word for word*
    Bien loialment, as I cowde me avise.   *'Very loyally'; discern*
    Than prayd I hir in every maner wise   *most earnestly*
90 That of hir name I myght have remembraunce.
    She sayde she was callid Perseveraunce.

---

[1] *Not only forget-me-not's, but remember-me's also*

So furthermore to speke than was I bold: *then*
Where she dwelt I prayed hir for to say.
And she ageyne ful curteisly me told:
95 'My dwellyng is and hath be many a day   *been*
With a lady.' 'What lady, I yow pray?'
'Of grete astate, thus warne I yow,' quod she. *I tell you for a fact*
'What calle ye hir?' 'Hir name is Loiaulte.'

'In what office stand ye, or in what degre?'   *rank*
100 Quod I to hir, 'that wold I wit ful fayne.' *would; gladly know*
'I am,' quod she, 'unworthy though I be,
Of hir chamber hir ussher in certayne;   *certainly*
This rodde I bere as for a tokene playne,
Lyke as ye knowe the rule in suche service
105 Perteyneng unto the same office.

She charged me be hir comaundement
To warne yow and youre felawes everichone
That ye shuld come there as she is present   *to where*
For a counsaile, whiche shuld be anone,   *council*
110 Or seven dayes bien comen and gone.   *Before; are*
And more she badde that I shuld sey   *And furthermore*
Excuse ther myght be none nor delay.

Another thyng was nygh forgete behynd *nearly forgotten in passing*
Whiche in no wise I wold nat but ye knewe —
115 Remembre it wele and bere it in your mynde:
Al youre felawes and ye must com in blewe,   *blue*
Everiche yowre matier for to sewe,   *petition; present*
With more, whiche I pray yow thynk upon,
Yowre wordes on yowre slevis everichon.   *mottoes; sleeves*

120 And be nat ye abasshed in no wise,
As many as bien in suche an high presence;   *Though many are*
Make youre request as ye can best devise
And she gladly wil yeve yow audience.   *give*
Ther is no grief nor no maner offence
125 Wherin ye fele your hert is displeased
But with hir help right sone ye shul bien eased.' *be*

35

'I am right glad,' quod I, 'ye telle me this;
But ther is none of us that knowith the way.'
'And of your wey,' quod she, 'ye shul nat mys;   *shall not go wrong*
130 Ye shul have one to guyde yow day be day
Of my felawes — I can no better say —
Suche on as shal telle yow the wey ful right;
And Diligence this gentil womman hight,   *is called*

A womman of right famous governaunce   *wise and discreet conduct*
135 And wele cherisshed, I sey yow for certeyne;   *held in great affection*
Hir felawship shal do yow grete plesaunce,
Hir porte is suche, hir manere is trewe and playne;   *demeanor*
She with glad chiere wil do hir busy peyne   *utmost exertion*
To bryng yow there. Farwele, now have I done.'
140 'Abide,' quod I, 'ye may nat go so soone.'

'Whi so?' quod she, 'and I have fer to go   *for I have far*
To yeve warnyng in many dyvers place   *give*
To youre felawes and so to other moo,   *others more*
And wele ye wote I have but litel space.'   *time to spare*
145 'Yit,' quod I, 'ye must telle me this cace,   *point*
If we shal any men unto us calle?'
'Nat one,' quod she, 'may come among yow alle.'

'Nat one?' quod I, 'ey, benedicite!   *oh, my goodness!*
What have they don? I pray yow, telle me that.'
150 'Now, be my lif, I trowe but wele,' quod she,   *by my life; believe*
'But evere I can beleve ther is somwhat,
And for to sey yow trowth, more can I nat;
In questions nothyng may I be to large,   *too open and unconstrained*
I medle me no further than is my charge.'   *get involved; responsibility*

155 'Than thus,' quod I, 'do me til undrestond   *give to me*
What place is there this lady is dwellyng?'
'Forsoth,' quod she, 'and on sought al a lond,   *even if one searched*
Feirer is none, though it were fore a kyng;
Devised wele, and that in every thyng;   *Well planned*
160 The toures high ful plesaunt shul ye fynde,
With fanes fressh tournyng with every wynde;   *weather vanes*

36

The chambres and parlours both of oo sort, *of the same kind*
With bay wyndowes goodely as can be thought,
As for daunsyng and other wise disport; *kinds of amusement*
165 The galaries right wonderfully wrought;
That wele I wote, yef ye were thider brought *if*
And toke good hede therof in every wise,
Ye wold it thynk a verray paradise.' *an absolute*

'What hight this place?' quod I, 'now sey me that.' *is called*
170 'Plesaunt Regard,' quod she, 'to telle yow pleyne.'
'Of verray trouth?' quod I, 'and wote ye what, *Indeed?; know*
It may wele be callid so sertayne. *certainly*
But furthermore this wold I wite ful fayne, *gladly*
What shal I do as soone as I com there
175 And after whom that I may best enquere?'

'A gentilwomman, porter at the yaate, *gate*
Ther shal ye fynde; hir name is Contenaunce. *Self-Control*
If so happe ye com erly or late, *whether it happens*
Of hir were goode to have som aqueyntaunce;
180 She can telle how ye shal yow best avaunce *put yourself forward*
And how to come to this ladyes presence;
To hir wordis I rede yow yeve credence. *advise; give*

Now it is tyme that I part yow fro, *from you*
For in goode soth I have grete busynesse.'
185 'I wote right wele,' quod I, 'that that is soo, *so*
And I thanke yow of youre grete gentilnesse; *courtesy*
Yowre comfort hath yeve me suche hardynesse *given; confidence*
That now I shal be bold withouten faile
To do after youre avise and counsaile.' *advice*

190 Thus parted she and I left al alone. *I remained*
With that I sawe, as I behielde aside, *to one side*
A womman come, a verray goodely oon,
And furth withal as I had hir aspied *And immediately*
Me thought anon that it shuld be the guyde;
195 And of hir name anon I did enquere.
Ful wommanly she yave this answere: *gave*

'I am,' quod she, 'a symple creature
Sent from the court; my name is Diligence.
As soone as I myght com, I yow ensure,   *assure*
200   I taried nat after I had licence,   *permission to leave*
And now that I am com to yowre presence,
Looke what service that I can do or may   *Whatever service*
Comaunde me, I can no further say.'

I thanked hir and prayed hir to come nere
205   Because I wold se how she were arrayed.
Hir gowne was bliew, dressed in goode manere   *adorned*
With hir devise, hir worde also, that sayde   *emblem; motto*
Taunt que je puis; and I was wele apayed,   *'As much as I can'; pleased*
For than wist I without any more   *knew*
210   It was ful triew that I had herd afore.

'Though we toke now before a lite space   *set off; little while*
It were ful goode,' quod she, 'as I cowth gesse.'   *could*
'How fer,' quod I, 'have we unto that place?'
'A dayes journey,' quod she, 'but litel lesse,
215   Wherfor I rede that we onward dresse,   *advise; proceed*
For I suppose oure felawship is past
And for nothyng I wold that we were last.'   *not for anything*

Than parted we at spryngyng of the day
And furth we wente a soft and esy pase,   *pace*
220   Til at the last we were on oure journay
So fer onward that we myght se the place.
'Nowe lete us rest,' quod I, 'a litel space,
And say we as devoutly as we can
A Pater Noster for seynt Julyan.'   *An 'Our Father'*

225   'With al myn hert,' quod she, 'I gre me wele;   *I heartily agree*
Moche better shul we spede whan we have done.'   *prosper*
Than taryed we and sayde it every dele.   *every bit*
And whan the day was fer gon after none
We sawe a place, and thider come we sone,
230   Whiche rounde about was closid with a wal
Semyng to me ful like an hospital.

There fonde I oon had brought al myn array,
A gentilwomman of myn acqueyntaunce.
'I have mervaile,' quod I, 'what maner wey
235   Ye had knowlache of al this governaunce?'   *knowledge; arrangement*
'Yis, yis,' quod she, 'I herd Perseveraunce,   *Yes, yes*
How she warned youre felawes everichone,
And what array that ye shal have upon.'

'Now, for my love,' quod I, 'I yow pray,
240   Sith ye have take upon yow al this peyne,   *Since; trouble*
That ye wold helpe me on with myne array,
For wite ye wele I wold be go ful fayne.' [1]
'Al this prayer nedith nat certeyne,'   *is quite unnecessary*
Quod she ageyne; 'com of, and hie yow soone,   *come on; hasten*
245   And ye shal se how wele it shal be done.'

'But this I dowte me gretely, wote ye what,
That my felaws bien passed by and gone.'
'I waraunt yow,' quod she, 'that ar they nat,
For here they shul assemble everichon.
250   Natwithstandyng, I counseil yow anone
Make ye redy and tarye ye no more;
It is non harme though ye be there afore.'

So than I dressid me in myn array
And asked hir if it were wele or noo.
255   'It is,' quod she, 'right wele unto my pay;   *to my satisfaction*
Ye dare nat care to what place so ever ye goo.'   *need not worry*
And while that she and I debated soo
Com Diligence, and sawe me al in bliew:
'Suster,' quod she, 'right wel broke ye your niewe.' [2]

260   Than went we forth and met at aventure   *by chance*
A yong womman, an officer semyng.   *by appearance*
'What is your name,' quod I, 'goode creature?'

---

[1] *Believe me I would gladly be gone*
[2] *'Sister,' she said, 'your new clothes suit you very well'*

	'Discrecioun,' quod she, 'without lesyng.'	*falsehood*
	'And where,' quod I, 'is yowre abidyng?'	*abode*
265	'I have,' quod she, 'this office of purchace,	*purchasing supplies*
	Chief purviour that longith to this place.'	*purveyor; belongs*

	'Faire love,' quod I, 'in al youre ordynaunce,	*organization*
	What is hir name that is the herbegyer?'	*lodgings-officer*
	'Forsoth,' quod she, 'hir name is Aqueyntaunce,	*Friendship*
270	A womman of right graciouse maner.'	
	Than thus quod I, 'What straungiers have ye here?'	
	'But fewe,' quod she, 'of hie degre ne lowe;	
	Ye bien the first, as ferforth as I knowe.'	*as far as*

	Thus with talis we com streyght to the yaate;	*chat; gate*
275	This yong womman departed was and gone.	
	Com Diligence and knokked fast therate.	
	'Who is without?' quod Contenaunce anone.	
	'Triewly,' quod she, 'faire suster, here is one.'	
	'Whiche oon?' quod she; and ther-withal she lough:	*laughed*
280	'I, Diligence, ye knowe me wele inough!'	

	Than opened she the gate and in we goo.	
	With wordis feyre she sayde ful gentily:	*courteously*
	'Ye ben welcom, iwis; bien ye no mo?'	*indeed*
	'No,' quod she, 'save this womman and I.'	
285	'Now than,' quod she, 'I pray yow hertily,	
	Take my chambre as for a while to rest	
	To yowre felawes bien comen, I hold it for the best.'	*Until*

	I thanked hir and furth we gon echeon	
	Til hir chambre without wordes mo.	*To; more*
290	Come Diligence and toke hir leve anon;	
	'Where ever yow list,' quod I, 'nowe may ye goo,	*it pleases you*
	And I thank yow right hertily also	
	Of yowre laboure, for whiche God do yow mede;	*reward*
	I can nomore, but Jhesu be yowre spede.'	*can say; help*

295   Than Contenaunce asked me anone:
       'Yowre felawship, where bien they now?' quod she.
       'Forsoth,' quod I, 'they bien comyng echeone,
       But in certeyne I knowe nat where they be.
       At this wyndow whan they come ye may se;
300   Here wil I stande awaityng ever among, [1]
       For wele I wote they wil nat now be long.'

       Thus as I stode musyng ful busily
       I thought to take heede of hir array.
       Hir gowne was bliew, this wote I verily,
305   Of goode facion and furred wele with gray; [2]
       Upon hir sleve hir worde, this is no nay,   *there is no denying it*
       The whiche saide thus, as my penne can endite,   *write*
       A moy que je voy, writen with lettres white.   *'To me what I see'*

       Than ferforth as she com streyght unto me,   *immediately as*
310   'Yowre worde,' quod she 'fayne wold I that I knewe.'
       'Forsoth,' quod I, 'ye shal wele know and se:
       And for my word, I have none, this is trewe;
       It is inough that my clothyng be blew
       As here before I had comaundement,
315   And so to do I am right wele content.

       But telle me this, I pray yow hertily,
       The stiward here, sey me, what is hir name?'
       'She hight Largesse, I say yow surely,   *is called Generosity*
       A faire lady and right of nobil fame;   *of truly noble*
320   Whan ye hir se ye wil report the same.
       And undir hir, to bid yow welcom alle,
       There is Bealchiere, the marchal of the halle.   *Good Cheer*

       Now al this while that ye here tary stille
       Yowre owne matiers ye may wele have in mynde;
325   But telle me this, have ye brought any bille?'   *petition*

---

[1] *Here I will stand, looking out every now and then*
[2] *Of good fashion and well-trimmed with gray fur*

'Ye, ye,' quod I, 'or ellis I were behynde;   *remiss*
Where is ther on, telle me, that I may fynde
To whom I may shewe my matiers playne?'   *openly*
'Surely,' quod she, 'unto the chambrelayne.'

330 'The chambrelayne,' quod I, 'say ye trewe?'
'Ye verily,' quod she, 'be myn advise,   *by my advice*
Be nat aferd but lowly til hir shewe.'   *humbly; make petition*
'It shal be don,' quod I, 'as ye devise,   *suggest*
But me must knowe hir name in every wyse.'   *in any case*
335 'Triewly,' quod she, 'to telle yow in substaunce,   *in short*
Without feyneng, hir name is Remembraunce.   *evasion*

The secretarye yit may nat be forgete,
For she may do right moche in every thyng;   *much*
Wherfor I rede whan ye have with hir met   *advise*
340 Yowre matier hole telle hir withoute feyneng;   *whole petition*
Ye shal hir fynde ful goode and ful lovyng.'
'Telle me hir name,' quod I, 'of gentillesse.'   *out of courtesy*
'Be my goode soth,' quod she, 'Avisenesse.'   *truth; Circumspection*

'That name,' quod I, 'for hir is passyng goode,   *extremely*
345 For every bille and cedule she must se.   *written petition*
Now, goode,' quod I, 'com stonde where I stoode;   *good lady*
My felawes bien comyng, yonder they be.'
'Is it a jape, or say ye soth?' quod she.
'In jape? nay, nay! I say it for certeyne;
350 Se how they come togyder tweyne and tweyne.'   *two by two*

'Ye say ful soth,' quod she, 'it is no nay;   *it cannot be denied*
I se comyng a goodely company.'
'They bien,' quod I, 'suche folk, I dare wele say,
That list to love, thynk it ful verily,   *That desire; believe*
355 And my faire love, I pray yow feithfully,
At any tyme whan they upon yow cal,
That ye wil be goode frend to theym al.'

'Of my frendship,' quod she, 'they shul nat mys,
As for ther case to put therto my payne.'   *utmost exertion*
360   'God yield it yow,' quod I; 'but telle me this: *repay*
How shal we knowe whiche is the chambrelayne?'
'That shal ye wele knowe by hir worde certayne.'   *truly*
'What is hir worde, suster, I pray yow say?'
'*Plus ne purroy*, thus writeth she alway.'   *'I could [do] no more'*

365   Thus as we stoode to-gydre, she and I,
At the yate my felawes were echon.
So mette I theym, as me thought was goodely,   *polite*
And bad hem welcom al by one and oon.   *one by one*
Than forth com Contenaunce anon:
370   'Ful hertily, feyre sustres al,' quod she,
'Ye bien right welcom to this contre.

I counseile yow to take a litel rest
In my chambre, if it be youre plesaunce.
Whan ye bien there me thynk it for the best
375   That I gon in and cal Perseveraunce
Because she is oon of youre acqueyntaunce,
And she also wil telle yow every thyng
How ye shal be rulyd of your comyng.'   *concerning your arrival*

My felawes al and I, be oon avise,   *by unanimous judgment*
380   Were wele agreed to do as she sayde.
Than we began to dresse us in oure guyse   *our appointed attire*
That folk shuld se us nat unpurvayde,   *unprovided for*
And wageours among us there we layde
Whiche of us atired were goodeliest
385   And whiche of us al preysed shuld be best.

The porter than brought Perseveraunce;
She welcomd us in ful curteys manere:
'Thynk ye nat long,' quod she, 'youre attendaunce;   *consider; wait*
I wil go speke unto the herbergier   *lodgings-officer*
390   That she may purvey for youre loggyng here,   *provide*
Than wil I gon to the chambrelayne
To speke for yow, and come anon agayne.'

And whan she departed and was agone
We sawe folkes comyng without the wal,
395   So grete people that nombre couthe we none. [1]
Ladyes they were and gentil wymmen al
Clothed in bliew everiche, her wordes withal;   *with their mottoes too*
But for to knowe theyr wordis or devise
They com so thycke we myght in no wise.

400   With that anon come Perseveraunce
And wher I stoode she com streight to me:
'Ye bien,' quod she, 'of myn old acqueyntaunce,
Yow to enquere the bolder dare I be
What worde they bere eche after theyr degre;   *rank*
405   I pray yow telle it me in secrete wise
And I shal kepe it close on warantise.'   *I guarantee*

'We bien,' quod I, 'fyve ladies al in feere,   *all in company*
And gentil wymmen foure in company;
Whan they begynne to opyn theyr matiere
410   There shal ye knowe her wordis, by and by.   *their; one after another*
But as for me I have none verily
And so I told to Countenaunce here afore;
Al myn array is bliew, what nedith more?'

'Now,' quod she, 'I wil go in agayne,
415   That ye may know what ye shal do.'
'Forsoth,' quod I, 'yif ye wil take the peyne,
Ye dide right moche for us, yif ye did so;
The rather spede the sonner may we go. [2]
Grete cost alwey there is in taryeng,   *Great harm*
420   And long to sue it is a wery thyng.'

Than parted she and come agayne anon:
'Ye must,' quod she, 'com to the chambrelayne.'
'We bien,' quod I, 'now redy, everichone,

---

[1] *So many people that we had no notion of the number*
[2] *The sooner dealt with, the sooner we may depart*

To folowe yow whan ever yow list, certeyne.
425   We have none eloquence, to telle yow pleyne,
Besechyng yow we may be so excused
Oure triewe meanyng that it be nat refused.'

Than went we forth after Perseveraunce.
To se the prease it was a wonder case;   *throng; wonderful thing*
430   There for to passe it was grete combraunce,   *inconvenience*
The people stoode so thykk in every place.
'Now stonde ye stille,' quod she, 'a litel space,
And for yowre ease somwhat shal I assay
Yif I can make yow any better way.'

435   And furth she goth among hem everychon,
Makyng a wey that we myght thurgh passe
More at oure ease, and whan she had don
She bekened us to com ther as she was,
So after hir we folowed more and lasse.   *one and all*
440   She brought us streight unto the chambrelayne;
There left she us and than she went agayne.

We salwed hir as reson wold it soo,   *greeted*
Ful humbly besechyng hir goodenesse,
In oure matiers that we had for to doo,
445   That she wold be goode lady and maystresse.
'Ye bien welcom,' quod she, 'in sothfastnesse,   *certainty*
And so what I can do yow for to please
I am redy, that may be for youre ease.'

We folowed hir unto the chambre doore;
450   'Suster,' quod she, 'come in ye after me.'
But wite ye wele, ther was a paved floore,
The goodeliest that any wight myght see;   *person*
And furthermore aboute than loked we
On eche a corner and upon every wal,
455   The whiche is made of berel and cristal;   *beryl*

45

Wheron was graven of storyes many oon: *engraved*
First how Phillis of wommanly pite   *because of*
Deyd pitously for the love of Demephon;   *Died*
Next after was the story of Thesbe,
460 How she slowe hir self under a tre;   *slew*
Yit sawe I more how in pitous case
For Antony was slayne Cleopatrace;

That other syde was how Melusene
Untriewly was disceyved in hir bayne;   *deceived; bath*
465 Ther was also Anelada the quene
Upon Arcite how sore she did complayne;
Al these storyes wer graven ther certayne
And many mo than I reherce yow here —   *recount*
It were to long to telle yow al in feere.   *too; completely*

470 And bicause the wallis shone so bright
With fyne umple they were al over-spredde   *gauze*
To that entent folk shuld nat hurt theyr sight,
And thurgh that the storyes myght be redde.
Than further I went as I was ledde
475 And there I sawe without any faile
A chayer set with ful riche apparaile;   *adornment*

And fyve stages it was set from the grounde,   *steps*
Of cassidony ful curiously wrought,   *chalcedony; intricately*
With foure pomels of gold and verray rounde   *knobs; completely*
480 Set with saphirs as fyne as myght be thought.
Wote ye what, yif it were thurgh sought   *if; thoroughly searched*
As I suppose from this contre til Ynde,   *India*
Another suche it were hard to fynde.

For wete ye wele, I was ful nere that,   *know you well*
485 So as I durst beholdyng by and by.   *every detail in turn*
Above ther was a riche cloth of state   *canopy*
Wrought with the nedil ful straungely,   *unusually*
Hir worde theron, and thus it sayde triewly:
A Endurer, to telle in wordis fewe,   *'[Ever] to endure'*
490 With grete lettres, the better for to shewe.   *capital*

Thus as we stoode a doore opened anon;
A gentil womman semely of stature,   *comely*
Beryng a mace, com out, hir self alone —
Triewly, me thought, a goodely creature.
495   She spak nothyng to lowde, I yow ensure,   *too*
Nor hastily, but bi goodely warnyng: *with polite warning*
'Make roome,' quod she, 'my lady is comyng.'

With that anon I saw Perseveraunce
How she hield up the tappet in hir hande.   *held; cloth-hanging*
500   I sawe also in right goode ordynaunce   *orderly fashion*
This grete lady withyn the tappet gan stande,
Comyng outward, I wil ye undrestande,
And after hir a noble company,
I cowde nat telle the nombre sikerly.   *for certain*

505   Of theyr names I wold nothyng enquere
Further than suche as we wold sue unto,
Sauf oo lady whiche was the chaunceler —   *Except for one*
Attemperaunce, sothly, hir name was soo —   *Temperance*
For us must with hir have moche to doo
510   In oure matiers and alwey more and more.
And so furth to telle yow furthermore:

Of this lady hir beauties to discryve   *describe*
My konnyng is to symple verily,   *skill*
For never yit the dayes of al my live   *life*
515   So inly fayre I have none sene triewly,
In hir astate assured utterly;   *noble state*
Ther lakked naught, I dare yow wele ensure,
That longged to a goodely creature.   *was appropriate*

And furthermore to speke of hyr aray
520   I shall yow tell the maner of hyr goune:
Of cloth of gold full ryche, hyt ys no nay,
The colour blew of a ryght good fassion,   *blue; fashion*

47

In taberd wyse, the slevys hangyng don; [1]

And what purfyll ther was and in what wyse   *embroidered hem*

525   So as I can I shall hyt yow devyse.   *describe*

Aftyr a sort the coler and the vent, [2]

Lyke as ermyn ys made in purfelyng,   *used in trimming borders*

With gret perles full fyne and oryent   *precious*

They were couchyd all aftyr oon worchyng [3]

530   With dyamondes in stede of pouderyng;   *'powdering' with ermine tails*

The slevys and purfyllys of assyse,   *sleeves; fur-trim; fashion*

They were made lyke in every wyse;   *in the same style*

Abowte hir nekke a serpe of fayre rubies   *neck-ring*

In white floures of right fyne enemayle;

535   Upon hir hede sette in the fresshest wise

A cercle with grete balays of entaile;   *diadem; ruby with engraving*

That in ernest to speke, withouten faile,

For yong and old and every maner age

It was a world to loke on hir visage.   *supreme delight*

540   This comyng to sit in hir astate,   *This [lady] having come*

In hir presence we knelid downe echeon

Presentyng up oure billis and, wote ye what,

Ful humbly she toke hem by oon and oon.

Whan we had don than com they al anon

545   And dide the same iche after in theyr manere,

Knelyng attones and risyng al in feere.   *at the same time; together*

Whan this was don, and she sette in hir place,

The chambrelayne she dide unto hir cal,

And she goodely comyng til hir a-pace   *with brisk stride*

550   Of hir intent knowyng nothyng at al:

'Voyde bak the prease,' quod she, 'unto the wal;   *Remove; throng*

---

[1] *In the style of a herald's coat, the sleeves hanging down*

[2] *According to the same pattern, the collar and the neck*

[3] *They were studded all according to a single design*

Make larger rome, but loke ye do nat tarye,
And take these billes unto the secretarye.'

The chambrelayne dide hir comaundement
555 And come ageyne as she was bode to doo;   *bidden*
The secretarie there beyng present
The billes were delyvered til hir also,
Nat only oures but many another moo.
Than this lady with gode avise ageyne   *discernment*
560 Anone withal callid hir chambrelayne.   *straightway with that*

'We wil,' quod she, 'the first thyng that ye doo,
The secretary make hir come anon
With hir billes, and thus we wille also,
In oure presence she rede hem everychone
565 That we may take goode avise theron   *advice*
Of the ladyes whiche bien of oure counsaile.
Looke this be don without any faile.'

The chambrelayn whan she wist hir entent
Anon she dide the secretary calle:
570 'Lete yowre billes,' quod she, 'be here present;   *presented*
My lady it wil.' 'Madame,' quod she, 'I shal.'   *wishes it*
'In hir presence she wil ye rede hem al.'
'With goode wil I am redy,' quod she,
'At hir plesure whan she comaundith me.'

575 And upon that was made an ordynaunce   *regulation*
They that com first theyr billes to be redde.
Ful gently than seyde Perseveraunce:
'Reason it wold that they were sonnest spedde.'   *soonest dealt with*
Anon withal upon a tappet spredde   *carpet*
580 The secretary layde hem downe everichon;
Oure billes first she red oon by oon.

The first lady, beryng in hir devise
Sanz que jamais, thus wrote she in hir bille: [1]

---

[1] *'Without ever [giving cause],' thus she wrote in her petition*

Compleyneng sore and in ful pitous wise
585 Of promesse made with feithful hert and wil
And so broken ayenst al maner skille,   *reason*
Without desert alweys in hir party,   *on her part*
In this matier desiryng remedy.

Hir next felawes word was in this wise —
590 *Une sans chaungier*, and thus she did compleyne: *'One without changing'*
Though she had bien gwerdoned for hir service,   *rewarded*
Yit nothyng, as she takith it, pleyne,   *fully*
Wherfor she cowde in no wise restreyne
But in this case sue until hir presence,   *unto*
595 As reason wold, to have recompence.

So furthermore to speke of other tweyne:
Oon of hem wrote after hir fantasye   *fancy*
Oncques puis lever, and for to telle yow pleyne,   *'I can never rise'*
Hir compleynt was grevous verily
600 For as she sayde ther was grete reason why,
And as I can remembre that matiere
I shal yow telle the processe al in fere. [1]

Hir bille was made compleyneng in her guyse   *in her fashion*
That of hir joye, comfort and gladnesse
605 Was no suerte, for in no maner wise   *certainty*
She fonde therin no poynt of stabilnesse, [2]
Now ill now wele, out of al sikernesse;   *security*
Ful humble desiryng of her grace   *humbly*
Som remedy to shewe in this case.   *offer*

610 Hir felaw made hir bille, and thus she sayde
In pleyneng wise: ther as she lovid best,
Whethir she were wroth or ill apayde,   *pleased*
She myght nat se whan she wold faynest,
And wroth was she in verray ernest

---

[1] *I shall give you a full account of the matter*
[2] *She discovered therein not the least bit of stability*

615 To telle hir worde, and forsoth, as I wote,
Entierment vostre right thus she wrote.   *'Entirely yours'*

And upon that she made a grete request,
With hert and wil and al that myght be done,
As until hir that myght redresse it best,   *unto*
620 For in hir mynde thus myght she fynde it sone
The remedy of that whiche was hir bone;   *request*
Rehersyng that she had seyd before,
Besechyng hir it myght be so no more.

And in like wise as they had don before
625 The gentil wymmen of oure company
Put up their billes; and for to telle yow more,
One of hem wrote *C' est sanz dire*, verily;   *'It needs no words'*
Of hir compleynt also the cause why
Withyn hir bille she put it in writyng,
630 And what it saide ye shul have knowlachyng.   *knowledge*

It sayde, God wote, and that ful pitously,
Like as she was disposed in hir hert,
No mysfortune that she toke grevously,   *took to heart*
Al on til hir it was the joy or smert;   *All one to her; pain*
635 Somtyme no thank for al hir desert;   *In the past no reward*
Other comfort she wayted non comyng,   *expected none to come*
And so used it greved hir nothyng;   *And being so used*

Desiryng hir and lowly hir besechyng
That she for hir wold se a bettir way,   *provide*
640 As she that had bien al hir dayes livyng   *As one*
Stadefast and triewe and so wil be alway.
Of hir felaw somwhat shal I yow say,
Whos bille was redde next after forth withal,   *forthwith*
And what it ment reherce yow I shal.   *recount*

645 *En dieu est* she wrote in hir devise,   *'In God is [my trust]'*
And thus she sayde, without any faile:
Hir trowth myght be take in no wise   *accepted as of value*

51

Like as she thought, wherfor she had mervaile,
For trowth somtyme was wont to take availe
650   In eche matiere, but now al that is goo —
The more pite that it is suffred soo.

Moche more ther was wherof she shuld compleyne
But she thought it to grete encombraunce   *burden*
So moche to write, and therfor, in certayne,
655   In God and hir she put hir affiaunce,   *trust*
As in hir worde is made a remembraunce,
Besechyng hir that she wold in that case
Shewe til hir the favour of hir grace.

The thridde she wrote rehersyng hir grevaunce,
660   Yee, wote ye what, a pitous thyng to here,   *Yea*
For as me thought she felt grete displesaunce —
One myght wele perceyve bi hir chiere,
And no wonder, it sat hir passyng neere;   *affected her very deeply*
Yit loth she was to put it in writyng,
665   But neede wil have his cours in every thyng.   *necessity; its way*

Sejour ensure this was hir worde certeyne,   *'Rest assured'*
And thus she wrote but in litel space:
There she loved hir labour was in vayne
For he was sette al in another place;
670   Ful humble desiryng in that cace   *humbly*
Som goode comfort hir sorow to appese
That she myght live more at hertis ease.

The fourth surely, me thought, she liked wele,   *was well pleased*
As in hir port and in hir havyng,   *demeanor; behavior*
675   And *Bien monest*, as ferre as I cowth feele,   *'Well advised'; perceive*
That was hir worde, til hir wele belongyng;
Wherfor til her she prayde above al thyng,
Ful hertily, to say yow in substaunce,   *in short*
That she wold sende hir goode contenuaunce.

680   'Ye have rehersed me these billis alle,
But now late se somwhat of youre entente.'

52

'It may so happe peraventure ye shal.'   *perhaps*
'Now, I pray yow, while I am here present.'
'Ye shal, parde, have knowlache what I ment;   *indeed*
685 But thus I say in trowth, and make no fable,
The case it silf is inly lamentable,   *itself; deeply*

And wele I wote that ye wil thynk the same
Like as I say whan ye han herd my bil.'
'Now, goode, telle on, I hate yow, be seynt Jame.' *good lady; bid*
690 'Abide a while, it is nat yit my wil;
Yet must ye wite, bi reason and bi skil,   *according to reason*
Sith ye knowe al that hath be done afore.'
And thus it sayde, without any more:

'Nothyng so lief as death to come to me   *dear*
695 For fynal end of my sorwes and peyne;
What shuld I more desire, as seme ye —   *think*
And ye knewe al aforne it for certeyne   *If*
I wote ye wold; and for to telle yow pleyne,
Without hir help that hath al thyng in cure   *in her care*
700 I can nat thynk that it may long endure;

And for my trouth, preved it hath bien wele —   *tested*
To sey the soth, it can be no more —
Of ful long tyme, and suffred every dele   *everything*
In pacience and kept it al in store;   *suffered it all in silence*
705 Of hir goodenesse besechyng hir therfor
That I myght have my thank in suche wise   *requital*
As my desert deservith of justice.'

Whan these billes were redde everichone
This lady toke goode avisement,   *consideration*
710 And hem til aunswere, eche on by oon,   *them*
She thought it to moche in hir entent,   *too*
Wherfor she yaf in comaundement
In hir presence to come both oon and al
To yeve hem there hir answere in general.   *collectively*

715 What did she than, suppose yow, verily?
     She spak hir silf and seyde in this manere:
     'We have wele sen youre billis by and by   *one by one*
     And som of hem ful pitous for to here.
     We wil therfor ye knowen this al in feere: *all together*
720 Withyn short tyme oure court of parlement
     Here shal be holde in oure paleys present,   *held in this very palace*

     And in al this wherein ye fynde yow greved
     There shal ye fynde an open remedy,
     In suche wise as ye shul be releved
725 Of al that ye reherce heere triewly.
     As of the date ye shal knowe verily,
     Than ye may have a space in your comyng,   *time to get here*
     For Diligence shall bryng it yow bi writyng.'

     We thanked hir in oure most humble wise,
730 Oure felawship echon bi on assent,   *with one accord*
     Submyttyng us lowly til hir servise,
     For as us thought we had oure travel spent   *labor*
     In suche wise as we hielde us content.
     Than eche of us toke other by the sleve,
735 And furth withal, as we shuld take oure leve.   *And that straightway*

     Al sodainly the water sprang anone
     In my visage and therwithal I woke.
     'Wher am I now?' thought I, 'al this is goon,'
     Al amased; and up I gan to looke.   *bewildered*
740 With that anon I went and made this booke,
     Thus symply rehersyng the substaunce   *essentials of the story*
     Because it shuld nat out of remembraunce,

     'Now verily your dreame is passyng goode
     And worthy to be had in remembraunce,
745 For though I stande here as long as I stoode
     It shuld to me be none encombraunce,   *burden*
     I toke therin so inly grete plesaunce.   *truly*
     But tel me now what ye the booke do cal,
     For me must wite.' 'With right goode wil ye shal:

750 As for this booke, to sey yow verray right   *absolutely correctly*
     And of the name to tel the certeynte,
     "La semble de Dames", thus it hight;   *'The Assembly of Ladies'*
     How thynk ye that the name is?' 'Goode, parde!'   *indeed*
     'Now go, farwele, for they cal after me,
755 My felawes al, and I must after sone.'
     Rede wele my dreame, for now my tale is done.

Notes

1–3   The autumn opening is rare in comparison with the spring opening (as in *FL*), but was developed because of its appropriateness to rather sad and somber poems (like *AL*).

8   *foure*: Thynne, in the first print of *AL*, changed this to *fayre*, presumably because lines 10–11 obviously refer to more than four. But he was wrong, and we must assume that all nine of the *felawship* are there spoken of. The matter is made clear at line 408 and by the sequence of petitions at lines 582–623 and 624–79. There was a fine but clear social distinction between *ladyes* and *gentil wymmen*.

10   *crosse aleys*: These sanded alleys, bordered by low rails (see line 42), came to be laid out with greater symmetry in the fifteenth century; here the cross-wise layout forms a kind of maze (see line 17). There is a very similar scene, with a group of ladies walking in a garden with 'rayled . . . aleyes,' in Chaucer's *Troilus*, II.813–26.

15   *Whereof I serve?*: The blurring of direct into indirect speech is common in Middle English poetry. The sense of the question, 'What are you doing here?' is, less politely, 'What is your function (office, purpose)?'

17   *mase*: Mazes became increasingly popular with the formalization of gardens in the late Middle Ages. They also became more difficult to negotiate, with hedges between the alleys (as at Hampton Court) rather than low rails that could be stepped over, as here (see line 42).

22   *must me wite*: This impersonal use of *must* with personal object, 'it is necessary for (me) to' (also 74, 334, 509, 749), seems a peculiar favorite of the poet of *AL*, though not common elsewhere.

48   *herber*: See *FL* 49n.

55   *tornyng whele*: It is not quite clear what feature of the *herber* is here referred to, whether a spiral staircase, a turnstile, or a circular flower-stand (like a sundial).

56   *margoleyne*, etc.: All the flowers in the arbor are emblematic, some by their very names, of serious and constant love.

68   *streames*: jets of water issuing from natural spring-heads (ingeniously concealed, line 70) and led through conduits about the garden, in this case to one side of the arbor and below floor level (*underneth*).

83   *blewe*: The wearing of blue is emphasized throughout the poem because blue was traditionally the color of truth and fidelity, especially as opposed to green (see *FL* 329n).

85–86   *enbrowdid*: There is abundant testimony in France and England in the fifteenth century to the practice of embroidering garments with devices or emblems, especially flowers.

87–88   *hir word*: Mottoes, usually in French, were also frequently embroidered on garments, especially on the hems of wide hanging sleeves (see 119). This kind of ornamentation had a rich symbolic language of its own in the 'game of love'; such mottoes are quite different from family mottoes, being intended as an ingenious form of mystification and not for identification. The mottoes in *AL* (88, 208, 308, 364, 489, 583, 590, 598, 616, 627, 645, 666, 675) belong to no known historical persons, and were probably made up for the purposes of the poem.

102   *ussher*: The Usher of the Chamber looked after the food and service in the lord's room. Distinctions of rank and status (see 99) were carefully observed in a lord's household, and the carrying of a staff of office (see 103–05) was a jealously guarded privilege.

148   *benedicite*: Literally, 'bless ye (the Lord)!'

163   *bay wyndowes*: This is the first recorded use of the term in a literary text. One of the earliest buildings to have bay windows was the palace of Humphrey, Duke of Gloucester, at Plesaunce, near Greenwich.

165 *galaries*: sheltered walks along the side of a house, partly open at the sides, like a monastic cloister.

170 *Plesaunt Regard*: the allegorical reference (buildings often have such names in love-vision poetry) is to the pleasant aspect of a lady towards one who pleases her (cf. *Swete-Lokyng* in Chaucer's *Romaunt of the Rose* 2896), but it is easy to see how the name might be thought appropriate to the building itself (see 171–72).

224 *seynt Julyan*: a prayer for good lodging for the night, to St. Julian the Hospitaller, patron saint of hospitality. After accidentally killing his parents, Julian set up a hospital to harbor poor people, and bore travelers across a nearby river as a penance.

231 *hospital*: In the Middle Ages the monastic and military-religious orders set up 'hospitals' for the accommodation of poor travelers and pilgrims, for the sick, aged, and insane, and for lepers. The reference to the *wal* (230) is reminiscent of the high continuous walls surrounding leper hospitals.

322 *marchal of the halle*: An important functionary of the household, responsible for the arrangement of ceremonies, especially the ordering and serving of guests at banquets.

325 *bille*: The usual word in fifteenth-century literature for a written petition or a statement of complaint, especially one concerning faithless or unrequited love, but there is much in *AL*, in the administrative arrangements for the presentation of the bills and in the bills themselves, to suggest that the poet is aware too of the stricter legal sense of the word and is making some attempt to imitate current legal procedure. In law, as in *AL*, the bill was the initiatory action of all procedure in equity; it consisted of a statement of complaint and a prayer for redress; it tended to be vague in point of fact but vehement in presenting the enormity of the offense; it was written in semi-legal parlance, with a profusion of loosely related participles and a convoluted syntax. Closest to *AL* in point of style are bills presented to the King's Council, which, like the court of Lady Loyalty, was approached by suitors as the supreme authority, able to right wrongs of every kind.

337   *secretarye*: The main job of the secretary — to collect, read over, and read out (553, 564) the written bills — is strikingly reminiscent of the role of the Clerk to the King's Council.

419–20   A medieval audience would need little reminding of the notorious dilatoriness of the law, whether in civil or criminal actions.

443   *hir goodenesse*: One can see here how an abstract noun comes to be used as a form of title.

455   *berel and cristal*: The idea of walls of beryl (not the modern semi-precious stone, but a form of crystal) and crystal is a fantasy, reminiscent of Chaucer's *The House of Fame* and Lydgate's *Temple of Glass*, which in their turn form part of a descriptive tradition going back to the Book of Revelation, Chapter 21.

456   *graven*: Tapestries and painted cloths were much more common in domestic interiors (as distinct from churches) than mural decoration, but literary buildings are often embellished with murals, as in Chaucer's *The Parliament of Fowls* (284–94), and The Knight's Tale (1918–2074), and Lydgate's *Temple of Glass* (42–142). The crystal engravings of *AL* are an added touch of fantasy. The *storyes many oon*, as befits the allegory, are of love's martyrs, true and faithful women unfortunate or wronged in love. Chaucer often finds occasion for introducing such lists of unfortunate women, and his *The Legend of Good Women* is a systematic martyrology. Phyllis, Thisbe, and Cleopatra usually figure in Chaucer's lists, and he tells the stories of all three in the *Legend*.

457   *of wommanly pite*: The idea is that Phyllis's misfortunes were due to her first taking pity on Demophon when he was shipwrecked on the shores of her kingdom. See *Legend* 2394–2561.

460   *under a tre*: The mulberry tree figures importantly in the story of Pyramus and Thisbe.

462   *was slayne*: This rather misses the point of Cleopatra's suicide. For the medieval view of Cleopatra as one of love's martyrs, see *Legend* 580–705.

463   *Melusene*: The heroine of a well-known story, translated from the French in two English fifteenth-century versions, *Melusine* (ed. A. K. Donald, EETS, e.s. 68, 1895) and *Partenay* (ed. W. W. Skeat, EETS, o.s. 22, 1866). Melusine was under a spell and used to turn into a serpent from the waist down every Saturday. When she married Count Raymond, she made him promise not to try to find out where she went on Saturdays. She proved a true and faithful wife, and bore him ten children, but Raymond's curiosity finally got the better of him. He followed her one Saturday, hacked a hole with his sword in the door of the room where she used to lock herself, and found her in the bath with her serpent's tail. His betrayal of the secret brings about her perpetual damnation.

465   *Anelada*: from Chaucer's *Anelida and Arcite*, much of which is devoted to Anelida's *Compleynt*.

477   *stages*: Mandeville describes an elaborate throne set on seven 'degrees' or steps in the palace of Prester John (*Travels*, ed. P. Hamelius, EETS, o.s. 153, 1919, p. 183), very similar to the throne of Darius in the Alexander legend (see *Wars of Alexander*, ed. H. Duggan and T. Turville-Petre, EETS, s.s. 10, 1989, 3464–3519).

478   *cassidony*: chalcedony is a semi-transparent white quartz, which forms the third foundation of the New Jerusalem in Revelation 21:19, and is associated in the medieval lapidaries with authority.

480   *saphirs*: the most precious of all jewels in the lapidaries; they were a token of truth and constancy.

482   *Ynde*: India was, to the medieval imagination, the extreme limit of remoteness, as well as a symbol of fabulous splendor.

499   *tappet*: a piece of figured cloth used as a hanging over a door or doorway.

507   *chaunceler*: In medieval households, the chancellor was a very important official who supervised the running of the household and the estate.

523   *In taberd wyse*: The reference is to the *tabard*, the short sleeveless tunic (originally simply two panels of cloth joined over the shoulders) emblazoned

with armorial bearings, worn by heralds; but clearly the phrase here describes the development of the late fifteenth-century surcoat (see *FL* 141n) with wide openings below the arms and long hanging sleeves.

526–30 The hems of the garment were studded with rows of pearls instead of ermine fur, and 'powdered' (sprinkled, a heraldic term) with diamonds instead of little black ermine tails. The details of Lady Loyalty's costume-decoration are very close to what can be seen in paintings of the mid to late fifteenth century, especially from Flanders, and what can be deduced from wills and inventories of the time.

533 *serpe*: a serpentine collar or neck-ring of precious metal, chased out or engraved, and set with white enamel flowers, each with a ruby in the center. Charles of Orléans had a similar collar.

536 *balays of entaile*: a balas ruby (a delicate rose-red variety of the spinel ruby), with an engraved design, set in the front of the diadem.

665 Proverbial.

681 *youre*: Lady Loyalty addresses the narrator.

689 *seynt Jame*: St. James (the Greater), brother of St. John the Evangelist. His shrine at Compostella in northwestern Spain was the greatest place of Christian pilgrimage in the Middle Ages.

694 The narrator's 'bill' is the only one of which we hear the exact words, as it is read out by the secretary.

720 *parlement*: The same distinction between an *assembly* (see 752), for the preliminary hearing of complaints, and a *parliament*, to pass judgment and enact laws, seems to be made in *The Isle of Ladies* 1967–72.

720–28 The postponed judgment is a frequent convention in poems involving an assembly or debate (e.g., *The Owl and the Nightingale*, *The Parliament of Fowls*), though of course it was common enough in real life, in law as in politics.

736   *water*: Skeat suggested that the water was thrown in her face by her companion to wake her up; this seems rather drastic. Perhaps the spray from the fountain caught her face as her head nodded in sleep. Poets exercise considerable ingenuity in waking their dream-narrators from sleep.

740   *this booke*: She seems to move momentarily outside the fiction of oral retelling of her story, as happens not uncommonly in medieval narrative.

743   The lady's story (29–742) ends here, and the knight or squire who originally accosted her (line 15) speaks.

756   Punctuation here obliges an editor to decide that the narrator turns from her interlocutor to her reader. Cf. the ambiguity in 740.

The Isle of Ladies

Introduction

There are two manuscripts of *The Isle of Ladies* (*IL*): Longleat House MS 256, of the mid-sixteenth century, and British Library MS Additional 10303, somewhat later. The original composition of the poem probably dates back to late in the previous century. The poem was picked up by Thomas Speght, from a copy not very distant from Addit.10303, and included in his 1598 edition of *The Workes of Geffrey Chaucer*, where, tendentiously and unluckily called *Chaucer's Dreame*, it accompanied *The Floure and the Leafe* (*FL*) into the Chaucer canon. It remained in the canon until relegated to the apocrypha in Skeat's 1878 revision of Robert Bell's edition of Chaucer, though Henry Bradshaw had questioned its authenticity as early as 1866. It was Bradshaw, on a visit to Longleat House, who inspected the manuscript and attached a note in which he first gave *IL* its present title. Skeat accepted the title in *Chaucerian and Other Pieces* (1897), and so it became established. He did not include the poem in that volume, as he did *FL* and *AL*, because of its inordinate length.

Of the three early texts, it is accepted that the best is Longleat, though the spelling of that manuscript, even given that it is of the mid-sixteenth century, is that of a maniac. There is also much that is vague, obscure, and confused in the text, but it does not seem impossible that these defects may be the responsibility of the poet, not the scribe. The present text follows that of Jenkins (1980), though I have introduced a few minor changes, and also systematized the spellings *u/v* and *i/j* according to modern practice, simplified initial *ff* as *f*, and followed modern word-division. I am very grateful to Dr. Jenkins for letting me use his edition as copy.

Since *IL* is a long poem and its story, unlike those of *FL* and *AL*, quite complicated, it will be useful to have a brief summary of the narrative:

> The dreamer finds himself in a beautiful isle inhabited only by ladies. He is courteously but coolly received by their governess, an older lady, who tells him he will have to leave the isle, though they must wait for confirmation of this from their queen, who is about to return

from a journey. The queen at this point arrives, accompanied by the dreamer's lady and a knight. She explains the mission she has been on to secure the three magic apples that guarantee her subjects youth, beauty, and happiness, and tells how she found the apples in the hands of the dreamer's lady and was then abducted by the knight. In her distress she was succoured by the lady (with an apple) and then by the knight, now repenting his rashness, and they have brought her safely back to the isle. The knight, asked to explain his conduct, falls for distress into swoon and lamentation. He is gently ministered to by the queen, but with no suggestion that she returns his passion (1-692).

At this point the navy of the God of Love arrives: scorning the flimsy defenses of the isle, he advances upon the queen and her company, and demands why she treats his servant so cruelly. After shooting into her the arrow of love, he moves among the rest of the ladies, paying special attention to the dreamer's lady and recommending the dreamer to her as her servant. Having received a 'bill' from the queen, the God of Love announces that he will be there in the morning to receive the submission of the ladies to his service. The day come, he also requires that the queen and the lady accept the knight and the dreamer into their love and service. With this he leaves. So too does the lady, much to the distress of the dreamer, who jumps into the sea and gets hauled aboard her ship, where he is brought back to life by her promise of love (and an apple). As they are about to land, he wakes up (693-1310).

Falling asleep again, he finds himself back on the isle, where the queen and knight are making plans for their wedding ceremony. The knight returns to his own kingdom to complete his arrangements, but is distressed to find that circumstances do not permit him to do so in time to keep to the date he has promised for his return. In some apprehension he returns five days late, only to find that the whole company of ladies has decided they have been betrayed and that they have given their love to unworthy suitors; they are all resolved to mortify the flesh, keep vigil, and repent unto death. The queen and two-thirds of the company are already dead. The knight stabs himself. All are taken off to be buried in the chapel of an abbey of black nuns in the knight's kingdom. There, in the chapel, a wounded bird is healed by the seed from a plant brought by its fellows. The same plant proves efficacious with the queen and with the knight. All the ladies are restored to life, the wedding plans reinstated, and the dreamer's lady fetched from her land to complete the celebrations. The noise of the music at his own wedding wakens the dreamer, who prays that his lady may turn his dream into reality (1311-2208).

IL was long seen as an occasional poem and was speculatively attached to various betrothals, including those of John of Gaunt, Chaucer, and Henry V. It has been attributed to Lydgate and Sir Richard Roos as well as Chaucer. But in reality nothing is known of its author, except that he is likely to have come from the north midlands, nor of any occasion to which the poem might refer. Nothing indeed needs to be known, since the poem is perfectly transparent as an allegory of sexual repression and fulfillment. It is a dream of male desire, in which the skill of women in deflecting men's sexual drive with 'fayre wordes' (741), enigmatic smiles (883-92), and vague noncommittal promises (642-78), their skill in managing the world of mannered politeness, in which reputation or *name* is everything (see 529, 557, 1666), is overcome by the power of the God of Love, who operates here, as in the *Roman de la Rose*, exclusively to the furtherance of male sexual desire.

This allegory of power and the desire for sexual domination is what drives the poem, but it is softened and blurred with a multitude of subtle touches. For instance, the men of the poem, with the exception of the God of Love and the knight in his one unguarded moment (384), have thoroughly absorbed the rules of reputation — the care for *name*, the fear of slander and social disgrace — that the ladies use to protect their chastity. But more than this, the artificiality, fragility, and unnaturalness of the ladies' seclusion and refusal of love is suggested by the glass walls and elaborate artifice of the island's defenses, with their metal singing-birds and exotic carved flowers (78-84). The God of Love, on the other hand, is associated with real flowers and live singing-birds (707, 714, 952), and his presence seems to restore the natural flowers of the isle (841). The implication, of course, as throughout *Troilus and Criseyde*, is that it is men who know what women really want, though one might accept that there is potentially more to the contrast than this — something of what Yeats hinted at in *Byzantium* ('Miracle, bird or golden handiwork / . . . . scorn aloud / In glory of changeless metal / Common bird or petal / And all complexities of mire and blood'). The symbolism of birds and flowers is carried through into the startlingly beautiful climactic episode of the poem, where the bird that has been wounded (significantly enough in trying to escape through the chapel window), is brought back to life by the seeds from a miraculously rapidly growing plant provided by its fellow

(1864). It does not take much ingenuity to trace here the contrast between artificial and unnatural restraint and the life-giving force of natural love and compassion. There is an earlier suggestion of this at a key moment in the poem, when the queen is ministering to the distressed knight: she remains cool and noncommittal enough, in the way she feels ladies must, but there is 'a looke peteus / Of womanehed' (675-76) that she bestows upon him which does not seem part of her strategy, and which might be taken as just that opening of the heart to pity and love which *enables* the God of Love to make his entrance, as he does at this very moment.

Not everything in the poem is done so felicitously, and an unsympathetic inquiry would turn up lots of loose ends in the narrative. But in another respect, that is, in the presentation of the 'I' of the narrative, the poet has been very successful. The success is achieved by playing off two techniques of self-presentation one against the other. The first technique is to suggest a stumbling earnestness about the dreamer, and a desire that the audience should re-live with him his experiences (e.g., 36-42). His emotions are always overflowing into the narrative: the fear that creeps about his heart at his situation on the isle (257-62), his delight at seeing his lady made so much of (453), his excitement at the arrival of the God of Love's navy (705), his anxiety when the God of Love recommends him to his lady, fearing that she will think he has been talking to everyone (863), and his frank delight at the 'loaves and fishes' miracle of the embarkation (1560). At the very end of the poem, the translation of the 'Go little book' formula into an apostrophe to his own heart gives to the poem, instead of sealing it off as a 'book,' an urgent unfinished personal life. On the other hand, there is also a carelessly sophisticated mock-naiveté about the dreamer which makes us wonder, as we wonder with Chaucer, whether we have been taken in. There is self-conscious play with the conventions of the dream-poem, especially in the poem's prologue, where the recognition that he is having his dream at the time lovers conventionally have their dreams (54-55), the commendation of waking visions (like his) over dreams (43-59), and the demand that his rude style be tolerated (64), all stimulate our awareness of the artifice of the form. There is some humor too in the representation of the dreamer's experience, behavior, and reactions: not many will resist a smile when he is fished out of the water with boat-hooks after floundering out to his lady's boat (1159), nor when he describes his joy as being so great that all his bones desired to dance (1200-02). There are also moments when the dreamer stands momentarily outside the conventions of allegory or indeed of narrative itself, as when he explains, within the narrative, the exact allegorical significance of the ship the knight embarks in (1373), or refuses to reveal what he and his lady said in secret (1251-66). It is all a trifle brittle, and it is not Chaucer, but it gives a vitality to a form which is usually thought to have been on the point of exhaustion.

The poem's major weakness is the thinness of its stylistic texture and the diffuseness and vapidity of its syntax. Diffuseness is characteristic of medieval poetry written within the conventions of oral delivery, and it has its function, but there are degrees of diffuseness, and in *IL* there is remarkably little in the way of allusion, ornamentation, or metaphor to sustain poetic interest, and almost no power of visualization. As for the poet's sentences, it could be said, not uncharitably, that they operate not so much to drive towards a chosen meaning as to pump out clouds of verbiage that, it is hoped, will precipitate here and there as sense. It could be regarded as a poetic idiom of a kind, and it is certainly not unfamiliar to those who know Lydgate's systematically and self-consciously inflationary poetic techniques.

IL is different in many ways from *FL* and *AL*. It is not told by a woman-narrator, nor does it purport to be by a woman, and it has much more to do with the genre of romance, especially romances of Celtic origin such as the Breton *lais* of Marie de France (see e.g., 7ln, 340n, 1505n, 1864n), than those poems. But it makes an excellent complement to *FL* and *AL* in discussions of the fate of late medieval allegory and of the relationships between the sexes that are therein shadowed forth.

The Isle of Ladies

When Flora, the Quene of Pleasaunce,
Had hol acheved th' obessiaunce — *wholly; submission*
Of the freshe and new season
Thorowte every region,
5 And withe her mantell hol covert — *entirely covered*
That winter made had discovert, — *What winter had laid bare*
Of aventure, without light, — *By chance*
In May I lay uppon a nyght
Allone, and on my lady thowght
10 And how the Lord that her wrought
Couthe well entayle in imagerye [1]
And shewed had great masterye
When he in so litle space
Made suche a body and a face:
15 So great beawty, with suche features,
More then in other creatures. — *than*
And in my thowghtes, as I laye
In a lodge out of the waye,
Beside a well in a foreste,
20 Wher after huntinge I toke reste,
Nature and kynd so in me wrought — *natural disposition*
That halfe on slepe thay me browght,
And gan to dreme, to my thinkinge, — *And [I] began*
With minde of knowledge leke wakinge. — *like*
25 For what I dreamed, as me thought,
I sawe it, and I slepte nought.
Wherfore is yet my full beleve — *belief*
That some good spirite, that eve,
By maner of some cureux port — *mysterious mode of conveyance*
30 Bare me where I saw payne and sport. — *Bore*

---

[1] *Certainly knew how to carve a sculpted image*

But wether it were I woke or slept,
Well wot I oft I laught and wepte.
Wherefor I woll in remembraunce
Put hole the paine and the pleasaunce
35 Whiche was to me axes and heale.
Wold God ye wiste it every dele!
Or at the least ye might on night
Of suche another have a syght.
Althowghe it were to yow a payne,
40 Yet, on the morrowe, ye wold be fayne
And wishe it might longe duer.
Then might you saye ye had good eure!
For who that dremes and wenes he see,
Muche the better yet may hee
45 Wit what, and of home, and where,
And eke the lesse it wol him deare.
To thinke I se thus withe myne eyne!
Iwis this may no dreme bene,
But signe or signiffiaunce
50 Of hasty thinge, soundinge pleasaunce. [1]
For on this wise uppon a nyght,
As ye have hard, witheout light,
Not all wakynge ne full on slepe,
Abowte suche houre as lovers wepe
55 And cry after ther ladies grace,
Befell me this wonder case
Whiche ye shall here and all the wise
As holly as I cane devise
In playne Englishe, evell writton;
60 For slepe wrightter, well ye weten,
Excused is, thowghe he do mise,
More then on that wakinge is.
Wherefor, here, of your gentulnes
I you requier my boysteousnes
65 Ye let passe as thinge rude,
And hereth what I woll conclude;

Well I know; laughed
will
Recall all
both fever and health
Would to God; knew; bit
at night

glad
last
fortune
thinks; sees

Know; of whom
also; trouble
saw; eyes
Indeed

in this manner
heard
nor fully asleep

cry out for
wondrous adventure
all the manner of it
fully; can
badly written
sleep(y) writer; know
amiss
than one

lack of polish

---

[1] *Of an unforeseen matter having to do with pleasure*

	And of th' enditinge takethe no hede,	*art of composition take*
	Ne of the termes, so God you sped,	*rhetorical figures; prosper*
	But let all passe as nothinge were:	*as if it were of no account*
70	For thus befell as ye shall here.	
	Withein an ylle me thowght I was	*isle*
	Where wall and yate was all of glasse,	*gate*
	And so was closed rounde abowte	
	That leveles non come in ne owt:	*without permission; came*
75	Uncothe and straunge to beholde.	*Unfamiliar*
	For every yate of fine golde	
	A thousannd fannes ay turninge	*weather-vanes always*
	Entuned had, and birdes singinge	*Made to sound in tune together*
	Diverse, and on eche fanne a payer	*pair*
80	Withe open mouthe agayne th' ayer.	*to meet the air*
	And of a suite were all the towers	*in the same fashion*
	Sotilly carven after flowers	*Cleverly carved like*
	Of uncothe colours, duringe aye,	*strange; lasting ever*
	That never been none sene in May,	*none of them*
85	Withe many a smale turret highe.	
	But mane on lyve culd I non spye,	*a living man*
	Ne creatures save ladyes playe,	
	Wiche were suche of ther arraye	
	That, as me thowght, of godlyhed	*in fine appearance*
90	They passen all and womanhed.	*surpass*
	For to beholde hem daunce and singe	
	Hit semed like none earthely thinge,	
	Suche was ther uncoth countenaunce	*demeanor*
	In every playe of right usaunce. [1]	
95	And of one age everychon	*the same*
	They semed all, save only one	
	Wiche had of yeres sufficaunce;	*sufficiency*
	For she might neyther singe ne daunce,	
	But yet her countenaunce was as glad	
100	As she as few yeres had hadd	
	As any lady that was there;	

---

[1] *According to correct custom*

And as litle it did her dere — *put out*
Of lustines to laugh and tale — *pleasure; tell stories*
As she had full stuffed a male — *bag*
105 Of disport and new playes. — *fun; games*
Fayre had she been in her dayes,
And mistres semed well to be — *mistress*
Of all that lusty companye; — *pleasure-loving*
And so she might, I you ensure, — *assure*
110 For on the coningest creature — *one of the wisest of creatures*
She was, and so sayd everychone
That ever her knew, ther fayled none; — *not one disagreed*
For she was sobre and well avised, — *very judicious*
And from every fault disguysed, — *kept hidden*
115 And nothinge used but faythe and trothe. — *practised*
That she nas younge hit was great routhe, — *was not; pity*
For everywhere and in eche place
She governed her, that in grace
She stod alwaye withe pore and riche,
120 That, in a word, was none her liche, — *like*
Ne halfe so able misteres to be — *mistress*
To suche a lustye company.
Byfell me so, when I avised — *surveyed*
Had the yle, at me sufficed, — *that*
125 And hol th' astate everywhere — *all the state of things*
That in that lusty yle was there,
Wiche was more wonder to devise — *conceive*
Then the joieux paradise, — *joyful*
I dare well say; for flower, ne tree, — *nor*
130 Ne thinge wherein pleassaunce myght be,
Ther fayled none for every wighte; — *creature*
Had thay desyred day and nyghte
Richesse, hele, beauwty, and ease, — *health*
Withe everye thinge that hem might please,
135 Thynke, and have, hit cost no more. — *Think of it and you had it*
In suche a countrye there before
Had I not been, ne hard tell — *heard*
That lyves creature might dwell. — *living*
And when I had thus all abowght — *about*

71

140	The yle advised thorowghte	*surveyed thoroughly*
	The state and how they were arrayed,	*condition of things*
	In my harte I wex well payed,	*became well pleased*
	And in my self I me assured	
	That in my body I was well eured,	*in luck*
145	Sithe I might have suche a grace	*Since*
	To se the ladyes and the place	
	Wiche were so fayer, I you ensure,	
	That to my dome, thowghe that nature	*in my judgment*
	Wold ever strive and do hir payne,	*make her greatest effort*
150	She shuld not con ne mowe attaigne	*be able nor have power to*
	The lest feature to amende;	*least*
	Thowgh she wold all hir coninge spende	*skill*
	That to beawty might availe,	
	Hit were but payne and lost travayle:	*labor*
155	Suche parte in ther nativite	
	Was hem alarged of beawtie.	*generously granted*
	And eke they had a thinge notable	
	Unto ther deathe ay durable,	
	And was that ther beawte shuld dure,	*And that was; last*
160	Wiche was never seen in creature;	
	Save only ther, as I trowe,	*believe*
	Hit hathe not be wist ne know.	*Where it; been known*
	Wherefore I praise with ther coninge	
	That duringe bewte, riche thinge;	*enduring*
165	Had thay been of ther lyves certaigne,	
	Thay had been qwyt of every payne.	*released from*
	And when I wend thus all have seen,	*thought; to have seen*
	Th' estate, the riches, that might been,	
	That me thowght impossible were	
170	To se one thinge more then was there	
	That to beautie or glad coninge	*pleasing skill*
	Serve or avayle might ony thinge,	*any*
	All sodenly, as I there stode,	
	This lady, that couth so moche good,	*knew*
175	Unto me come withe smilinge chere	
	And sayd: 'Benedicite! This yere	*Bless ye!*

Saw I never man here but you.

Tell me how ye come hether nowe, *hither*

And your name, and were you dwell, *where*

180 And whom ye sek eke mot ye tell, *must*

And how ye come be to this place.

The soth well told may cause you grace; *truth*

And else ye mote prisoner be

Unto these ladyes here and me

185 That han the governaunce of this yle.'

And withe that word she gane to smyle,

And so dyd all the lusty rowte *company*

Of ladyes that stode her abowte.

'Madame,' quod I, 'this night paste,

190 Lodged I was and slepte faste

In a forest beside a well,

And nowe ame here. How shuld I tell?

Wot I not by whos ordinaunce, *whose command*

But only Fortunes purveaunce *forward planning*

195 Wiche puttes many, as I gesse,

To travell, payne, and busines, *labor*

And lettes nothinge for ther trowth *spares*

But some sleethe eke, and that is rowth; *slays; pity*

Wherefore I dowt hir britelnes, *fear; mutability*

200 Hir variaunce and unstedfastnes,

So that I am as yet affrayd *frightened*

And of my beinge here amayed; *dismayed*

For wondre thinge, semethe me,

Thus many freshe ladyes to see,

205 So fayer, so connynge, and so yonge, *clever*

And no mane dwellethe hem amonge. *man*

Wot I not how I hether come, *hither*

Madame,' quod I, 'this all and some. [1]

What shuld I feyne a longe processe *invent; story*

210 To you that seme suche a princes?

What please you comaunde or saye,

Here I am you to obeye

---

[1] *'Madam,' I said, 'This is the long and short of it'*

73

To my power, and all fulfill,
And prisoner byde at your will
215 Till you dewlye enformed be *properly*
Of everye thinge ye aske me.'
This lady ther right well appayed *pleased*
Me by th' ande toke and sayd: *hand*
'Welcome, prisoner adventurus! *unexpected*
220 Right glad am I ye have sayd thus.
And for ye doute me to displease, *fear*
I will assaye to do you ease.'
And with that word, ye anon, *yes indeed straightway*
She and the ladyes everychone
225 Assembled and to counsell went;
And after that, sone for me sent,
And to me sayd on this maner,
Word for word as ye shall here.

'To se you here us thinketh marvayle, *seems to us a marvel*
230 And how witheout boot or sayle *boat*
By any souttyllete or wyle *trickery*
Ye get have entre in this Ile. *have got entry*
But not for that, yet shall you see *nevertheless*
That we gentilwomen bee,
235 Lothe to displease any wight,
Notwithstondinge our great right.
And for ye shall well understand
The old custome of this lande
Wiche hathe continewed many yere,
240 Ye shall well wyt that withe us here
Ye may not byd, for causes twayne *stay*
Wheche we be purposed you to seyne. *say*

The ton is this: our ordinaunce, *The one*
Whiche is of longe continuaunce, *of great antiquity*
245 Woll not, sothely we you tell, *Desires*
That no mane here amonge us dwell;
Wherefore ye mot nedes retorne. *must*
In no weys may ye here sojorne. *way; remain*

74

	The tother is eke that our qwene	*The other*
250	Owt of the reme, as ye may sene,	*realm*
	Is, and may be to us a charge	*it may; harm*
	Yf we let you go here at large.	
	For wiche cause, the more we dowbte	
	To do a faute while she is owte,	*fault*
255	Or suffer that may be noysaunce	*what; harm*
	Again our olde acustemaunce.'	*Against; custom*
	And when I had these causes tweine	
	Herd, O God, whiche a payne	*Heard; what*
	All sodenly abowte my harte	
260	Ther come attons, and how smerte!	*at once; painfully*
	In crepinge soft, as who wold stele	*as if someone*
	Or me do robe of all myn hele;	*have robbed me; well-being*
	And made me in my thought so frayd	*afraid*
	That in corage I stode dismayed.	*spirit*
265	And standinge thus, as was my grace,	
	A lady come, more then apas,	*quite quickly*
	Withe huge pres hir abowte,	*throng*
	And told how the quene withoute	
	Was arryved and wold come in.	
270	Wele were thay that thether might wyn;	*Happy; thither*
	They hied so, they wold not byde	*hastened*
	The bridelinge of ther horse to ryde.	
	By ten, by six, by two, by thre,	
	Ther was not one abode with me.	*stayed*
275	The quene to mete, everychone	
	They went, and bod withe me not one.	*stayed*
	And I after, a softe paas,	*at a gentle pace*
	Imageninge how to purchace	
	Grace of the quene ther t' abyde,	
280	Till good fortune some happy guyde	
	Me send might, that wold me bringe	
	Where I was borne to my woninge;	*carried away; dwelling*
	For way ne sent knew I none,	*path*
	Ne whetherward I nyst to gone,	*did not know*
285	For all was see aboute the Ile.	*sea*

No wonder thowghe me lest not smyle,   *I had no wish to*
Seinge the case unquowth and straunge   *unfamiliar*
And so like a perelus chaunge.
Imageninge thus, walkinge allone,
290   I saw the ladyes everychone.
So that I myght somwhat ofer,   *offer*
Sone after that I drew me neare.
And tho I was war of the quene,   *then*
And how the ladyes on there knene   *knees*
295   Withe joyeuse wordes, gladly avised,   *devised*
Hir welcomed, so that hit sufficed
Thoghe she princes hole had bee   *entirely*
Of all that vironed is withe see.   *surrounded*
And thus avisinge with chere sadd,   *looking on; gloomy*
300   All sodenlye I wex gladd,   *became*
That greatter joye, as mot I thrive,   *may*
I trow had never mon on lyve   *believe; alive*
Then had I tho, ne harte more light,   *Than; then*
When of my lady I had syght
305   Wiche withe the quene come was there.
And in one clothinge bothe they were. [1]
A knyght also, right wel besene,   *very well trimmed out*
I sawe, that come was with the quene;
Of whom the ladyes of that Ile
310   Had huge wonder longe whyle,
Till at the last, right soberlye
The quene herselfe full coninglye   *wisely*
With softe wordes, in goodlye wyse,
Sayd to the ladyes yonge and wyse:

315   'My susters, how hit hathe befall,
I trow ye know it, on and all,
That of longe tyme here have I been
Withein this yle bydinge as quene,
Lyvinge at ease, that never wight
320   More perfyte joye have ne mighte;

---

[1] *They were both in the same style of clothing*

And to you been of governaunce   *in my way of governing*
Suche as ye fond in hol pleasaunce   *found entirely satisfying*
In every thinge, as ye knowe,
After our costome and our lowe.   *law*

325   Wiche how they first found were,
I trow ye wote all the manere   *believe; know*
And how who quene is of this Ile —
As I have bene longe while —
Yche seven yeres mot of usage   *must; ancient custom*

330   Visyt the hevenly armitage,   *hermitage*
Wiche on a roche so highe stondes
In strange se, out from all londes,   *sea; far from*
That to make the pillerenage   *pilgrimage*
Is caled a longe perileuse viage;   *journey*

335   For yf the winde be not good frind,   *friend*
The jorney duers to th' ende   *lasts*
Of hem that hit undertakes:
Of twenti thousande one not skapes.
Oppon whiche roche growethe a tree   *Upon*

340   That certayne yeres bares apples three,
Wiche thre apples who may have   *whoever*
Bene from all displeasaunce save   *safe*
That in the seven yere may fall.
This wote ye well, one and all.

345   For the first appull, and the hexst   *highest*
Whiche growethe unto you nexst,
Hathe thre vertues notable
And kepethe youthe ay durable,   *everlasting*
Bewtie and hele ever in one,   *health ever the same*

350   And is the beste in everychone.
The second appule, red and grene,
Only with lokes of your yene   *looks; eyes*
You nurrisshes in pleasaunce
Better then partrich ne fesaunce,   *pheasants*

355   And fedes every lyves wyght   *living creature*
Plesauntlye with the syght.
The thirde appule of the thre,
Wiche growethe loueste in the tree,   *lowest*

Who yt beres may not fayle
360 That to his pleasaunce may availe.   *Whatever*
So your pleasure and beutie riche,
Your duringe youthe ever liche,   *lasting; ever the same*
Your trothe, your coninge, and your welle,   *wisdom; well-being*
Hathe ay flowred, and your good hele   *happiness*
365 Witheout sicknes or displesaunce
Or thinge that to you was noysaunce,   *a harm*
So that you have as goddesses
Lived aboven all princesses.

Now is byfall as ye may see:
370 To gedre these sayd appuls three,   *To gather these same*
I have not fayled agayne the daye   *against (upon)*
Thetherward to take the weye,
Weninge to spede, as I had oft;   *Thinking to have success*
But when I come, I found aloft
375 My sister wiche that here stondes,
Havinge those appulles in her handes,
Avisinge hem, and nothinge sayde   *Looking at them*
But loked as she wer well payed.   *pleased*
And as I stode her to behold,
380 Thenkinge howe my joyes were cold
Sithe I those apples have ne might,
Even withe that, so come this knight,
And in his armes, of me unware,   *to me unexpectedly*
Me toke, and to his shipe me bare,   *carried off*
385 And sayd, thowgh he me never had sene,
Yet had I longe his lady bene,
Wherefore I shuld withe him wend,   *go*
And he wolde to his lives ende
My servaunte be, and can to singe   *began*
390 As one that had wone riche thinge.
Tho were my spirites fro me gone   *Then*
So sodenlye, everychone,
That in me appered but deathe;
For I feld neyther live, ne brethe,   *felt; life*
395 Ne good, ne harme, non I knewe.

The sodeyne paine me was so new,
That had not the hasty grace be   *immediate help been*
Of this lady, that fro the tree
Of her gentulnes so hiede
400   Me to comforthe, I had dyed;
And of her three applus, one
In myn hand ther put annone,
Wiche browght agayne minde and brethe,
And me recovered from the deathe.
405   Wherefore to her so am I holde   *beholden*
That for her all thinge do I wolde;
For she was leche of all my smart,   *physician; hurt*
And from great paine socourte myn harte,   *relieved*
And, as God wotte, right as ye here,   *knows*
410   Me to comforte, with frindlye chere   *friendly*
She did her power and her might;
And trewlye eke so did this knight,
In that he couthe, and oft sayd   *In whatever*
That of my woo he was il payed,   *ill pleased*
415   And cursed the shipe hem thether browght,   *the ship that*
The mast, the master that hit wrought.
And as eche thinge mot have an ende,   *must*
My suster here, our brother frinde,
Con withe her wordes so womanlye   *Began*
420   This knyght entreat and coningelye,   *skillfully*
For myn honour and his also,
And sayd that with her we shuld goo
Bothe in her shippe, where she was browght,   *wherein*
Wiche was so wonderfullye wrought,
425   So clene, so riche, and so arrayed
That we were bothe content and payed.
And me to comfort and to plesse,
And myn hart to put at easse,
She toke great payne in litle while,
430   And thus hathe browght us to this Ile
As ye maye se. Wherefore echone
I praye you thanke her, one and one,   *one after another*
As hertelye as ye cane devise

Or imagen in any wyse.'

435	At once ther, tho, men myght sene	
	A world of ladyes fall on knene	*knees*
	Before my lady, that ther abowte	
	Was left none stanndinge in the route,	*company*
	Bot all to th' erthe they went at once;	
440	To knele they spared not for the stones,	
	Ne for estate, ne for ther blode.	*their high birth*
	Well shewed they ther they cuthe moche good, [1]	
	For to my lady they made suche feaste,	
	With such wordes, that the leste	*least*
445	So frindlye and so faythefullye	
	Sayd was, and so coninglye,	
	That wonder was, seinge ther youthe,	
	To here the launguage they cothe,	*had command of*
	And holly how they governed were	*conducted themselves*
450	In thannkynge of my ladye there;	
	And sayd by will and maundement	*command*
	They were at her comandemente,	
	Wiche was to me as great a joye	
	As wininge of the towne of Troye	
455	Was to the hardye Grekes stronge	
	When thay yt wane with seage longe:	*won; siege*
	To se my ladye in suche a place	
	So receyved as she was.	
	And when they taled had a while	*talked*
460	Of this and that, and of the Ile,	
	My lady and the ladyes there,	
	All together as they were,	
	The quene herselfe begane to playe,	*speak playfully*
	And to the aged lady saye:	
465	'Now semethe you nat good it were, [2]	
	Sith we be all togither here,	*Since*

---

[1] *They well exemplified there that they knew exactly what was right*

[2] *Now doesn't it seem to you it would be a good idea*

To ordayne and avise the best *devise*
To set this knyght and me at rest?
For woman is a feble wyght *person*
470 To rere a ware agayne a knyght. *raise a war*
And sith he here is in this place
At my lyst, daunger or grace,[1]
It were in me great villanye *discourtesy*
To do him any tirrannye.
475 But fayne I wolde now, will ye here,
In his owne cunterye that he were,
And I in peace, and he at ease;
This were a waye us bothe to please.
Yf yt might be, I you beseche
480 Withe him hereof ye fall in speche.'
This lady tho began to smyle,
Avisinge her a littull whille, *Considering within herself*
And withe glad chere she sayd annon;
'Madame, I will unto him gone
485 And withe him speke, and of him fele *detect*
What he desyers, everye dele.' *every bit*
And soberlye this lady tho,
Herselfe and other ladyes two
She toke withe her, and with sad chere *with a serious face*
490 Sayd to the knyght on this maner: *in*
'Syr, the princesse of this Ile,
Whom for your pleasaunce many myle
Ye sowght have, as I understand,
Till at the last ye have her found,
495 Me sende hathe here, and ladyes twayne, *sent*
To here all thinge that ye sayne, *say*
And for what cause ye have her sowght,
Fayne wold she wyt, and hole your thought, *know, and all*
And whi you do her all this woo, *cause*
500 And for what cause ye be her foo, *enemy*
And whi, of everye wight unware, *unbeknown*
By force ye to your shippe her bare

---

[1] *According to my pleasure, [whether it be] disdain or favor*

81

That she so nyghe was agone   *was so nearly distracted*
That minde ne speche had she none,
505 But as a paynefull creature   *full of sorrow*
Diinge abode her adventure,   *awaited her fate*
That her to se enduer that payne,
I dare well saye unto you playne,
Right on yourselfe ye did amise,   *in*
510 Seeinge how she a princes is.'
This knyght, the whiche couth his good,   *knew what was good for him*
Ryght of his trothe meved his blood,   *drained (from his face)*
That pale he wox as any ledd   *lead*
And loked as he wold be dedd.
515 Blud was ther none in nayther cheke;
Wordles he was, and semed sike;
And so yt preved well he was,
For without mevinge any passe,   *moving a step*
All sodenlye, as thinge dyinge,
520 He fell at once downe sowninge;   *swooning*
That, for his wo, this lady frayed   *afraid*
Unto the quene her hied and sayd: *she hurried*
'Comethe on, anone, as have ye blisse!   *as you may have*
But be ye wyse, thinge is misse.   *Unless; amiss*
525 This knyght is ded or wil be sone;
Lo, where he lyethe yonde in sowne,   *swoon*
Without word or answeringe
To that I sayd have any thinge! [1]
Wherefore I dowbte that the blame
530 Might be hinderinge to your name,
Whiche flowred hathe so many yere
So longe, that for nothinge here
I wold in no wyse he dyedd.
Wherefore good were that ye hiedd   *it would be good*
535 His lyfe to save, at the lest;
And after that his woo be ceste,   *ceased*
Commaunde him to voyd or dwell,   *depart*
For in no wyse dare I more medell   *meddle*

---

[1] *To anything that I have said*

Of thinge wherein suche perill is
540　　As lyke is now to fall of this.'

　　　　This quene right tho, full of great feare,
　　　　Withe all the ladyes present there,
　　　　Unto the knyght come where he leye
　　　　And mad a lady to him saye:
545　　'Lo, here the quene! Awacke, for shame!
　　　　What will ye do? Is this good game?
　　　　Whi lye you here? Where is your minde?
　　　　Now is well sene your wyt is blinde,
　　　　To see so many ladyes here,
550　　And ye to make none other chere
　　　　But as ye sett them all at nowght.
　　　　Aryse, for His love that you bowght!'　　　　　　*redeemed*
　　　　But what she sayed, a word not one　　　　　　　*whatever*
　　　　He spake, ne answere gave her none.
555　　The quene of very pytye tho,
　　　　Her worshipe and his life also
　　　　To save, ther she dyd her payne,　　　　　*exerted herself*
　　　　And quocke for fere and con to sayne　　*quaked; and said*
　　　　For woo: 'Allas, what shall I do?
560　　What shall I saye this man unto?
　　　　Yf he dye here, lost is my name.
　　　　How shall I pleye this perilous game?
　　　　Yf any thinge be here amise,
　　　　Yt shal be sayd hit rigor is,　　　　　　　　　*cruelty is*
565　　Whereby my name enpayer myght,　　　　*might be injured*
　　　　And like to dye eke is this knyght.'
　　　　And withe that word, her hande she layed
　　　　Uppon his brest, and to him sayed:
　　　　'Awacke, my knyght! Lo, yt am I
570　　That to you speke! Now tell me whi
　　　　Ye fare thus and this payne enduer,
　　　　Seinge ye be in counterye suer,　　　　　　　*a safe country*
　　　　Amonge suche frindes that wold your hele,　*desire your well-being*
　　　　Your hartes ease eke, and your welle;
575　　And yf I wyst what you might ease

83

Or knew the thinge that you might please,
I you ensuer it shulde not fayle
That to youre hele you might avayle. *Whatever*
Wherefore with all myne harte I praye
580 Ye rysse, and lett us tale and pleye, *rise; converse*
And see how many ladyes here
Be common for to make you chere.' *Are come*

All was for nawght; for still as stone
He laye, and worde spake he none.
585 Longe while was or he might brayd, *ere; stir*
And of all that the quene had sayd
He wyst no worde; but at the last,
'Mercy' twies he cried faste,
That pyty was his voice to here
590 Or to beholde his paynefull chere,
Wiche was not fayned, well was to sene *as could clearly be seen*
Bothe by his visage and his eyne *eyes*
Wiche on the quene at once he caste,
And syghte as he wolde to-braste. *sighed; burst*
595 And after that he shright soo *shrieked*
That wonder was to se his woo;
For sythe that paine was first named *since*
Was never more woofull paine entamed, *revealed*
For withe voice ded he gan to playne, *dead*
600 And to himselfe these wordes sayne:
'I, woofull wyght full of maleure, *misfortune*
Am worse then ded, and yet I duer *endure*
Magre any payne or deathe; *Despite*
Agaynst my will I fele my brethe.
605 Whi ner I ded, sythe I ne serve *Why should I not be dead*
And sythe my lady will I sterve? *wishes that I die*
Where art thou, deathe? Art thou agast?
Well shall we mete yet at the laste!
Thowghe thou the hide, it is for nawght;
610 For, where thou dwell, thou shall be sought,
Magre thi subtill dowble face; *Despite*
Here will I dye, right in this place,

84

	To thi dishonour and myn ease.	
	Thi manner is no wyght to please.	*practise; creature*
615	What nedes the, sythe I the seche,	
	So the to hide, my paine to eche?	*increase*
	And well wyst thou I woll not lyve —	
	Who wolde me all this world here gefe —	*Even if someone; give*
	For I have withe my cowardice	
620	Lost joye, and helle, and my service,	*well-being*
	And made my soveraigne lady soo,	
	That while she lyves, I trow, my foo	*believe*
	She wil be ever to her ende.	
	Thus have I neyther joye ne frend.	
625	Wote I not whither hast or slowthe	*whether haste*
	Hathe caused this now, by my trothe;	
	For at the hermitage full hye,	
	Where I her saw first withe myn eye,	
	I hyed till I was alofte,	*hastened*
630	And mad my pace smale and softe,	*short and stealthy*
	Till in myn armes I had her faste,	
	And to my shipe bare at the laste;	
	Whereof she was displeased soo	
	That endles there semed her woo,	
635	And I thereof had so great feare	
	That me repent that I came there;	*I repent*
	Wiche hast, I trowe, con her displease	*haste; displeased her*
	And be the cause of my deseace.'	*And was; distress*
	And withe that word he can to crye	
640	'Now deathe, deathe!' twy or thrye,	*twice or thrice*
	A motird wot I not what of slougthe. [1]	
	And even withe that, the quene, of routhe,	*for pity*
	Him in her armes tooke and sayd:	
	'Now myn owne knyght, be not yll payed	*ill pleased*
645	That I a lady to you sente	
	To have knowledge of your entent;	
	For, in good faythe, I ment but well,	

---

[1] *He murmured I know not what (i.e., something inaudible) of dying*

	And wold ye wyst yt everye dell, [1]	*do [any harm]; indeed*
	Nor woll not do to you, iwysse.'	
650	And withe that word she can him kysse,	
	And prayed him ryse, and sayd she wold	*desired*
	His welfare by her trothe, and tolde	
	Him howe she was for his diseace	
	Right sorye, and fayne wold him please.	
655	His lyfe to save, thes wordes thoo	*these*
	She sayd to him, and many moo,	
	In comfortinge; for from the peyne	
	She wold he were delyvered fayne.	
	The knight tho upcast his eyne,	
660	And when he se it was the quene	*saw*
	That to him had those wordes sayde,	
	Ryght in his woo he can to brayd [2]	
	And him updressed for to knele,	*prepared*
	The quene avisinge wonder well.	*gazing upon*
665	But as he rosse, he over-threwe;	*rose; fell over*
	Wherefore the quene, yet eft newe,	*yet once again*
	Him in her armes annon toke	
	And piteuslye con on him looke.	
	But, for all that, nothinge she sayde,	
670	Ne spake not lyke she were well paied,	
	Ne no chere mad more sadd ne lyght,	*neither more*
	But all in on, to every wyght,	*equally combined*
	Ther was sene connynnge withe estate	*politeness with nobility*
	In her, witheout noyse or debate;	
675	For, save only a look peteus	
	Of womanehed, undispiteous,	*free from scorn*
	That she shewed in countenaunce,	
	Far semed her hart from obeysaunce.	*submission*
	And not for that, she did her paine	*notwithstanding that*
680	Him to recover from the paine,	
	And his harte to put at large.	*set free*
	For her entent was to his barge	

---

[1] *And really wanted you to know that*

[2] *So in the midst of his distress he stirred*

	Him to bringe agenst the eve,	*towards evening*
	Withe sertayne ladyes, and take leve,	
685	And pray him of his gentulnes	
	To suffer her thenceforthe in peace	*allow her [to live]*
	As other princisse had byfore;	*princes*
	And from thenseforthe, for evermore,	
	She wold him worshipe in all wise	
690	That jentylnes myght devise,	*courtesy; stipulate*
	And payne her holly to fulfill,	
	In honor, his pleasure and will.	

	And duringe thus the knyghtes woo —	
	Present the quene and other mo,	*The queen being present*
695	My lady and many another wight —	
	Ten thousand shippes, at a syght,	
	I sawe come over the wavy floude	
	Withe sayle and ore, thatt, as I stoode	
	Them to beholde, I cone marvell	
700	From whense myght come so many a sayle;	
	For sythe the tyme that I was bore,	
	Suche a navy ther before	
	Had I not sene, ne so arrayed,	
	That for the syght myn hart played	
705	Two and fro withein my brest	*To and fro*
	Fro joy; longe was or it wold rest.	*it was a long time before*
	For ther wer sayles full of flowers,	
	Aftercastelles withe huge towers,	*Stern-castles*
	Seminge full of armes bright,	*coats of arms (weapons?)*
710	That wonder lusty was the syght,	*invigorating*
	Withe large toppes and mastes longe,	*mast-head platforms*
	Richelye depainte; and ever amonge,	*ever and again*
	At certen tymes, con repayer	*made their way*
	Smale burdes downe from the eyor,	*air*
715	And on the shippes bordes abowte	*planks*
	Sate, and songe withe voice full owt	*full-throated*
	Ballades and leyes, right joyouslye,	*lays*
	As they couthe in ther armonye;	
	That you to wright that I ther see,	*write what; saw*

720 Myn excuse is it may not bee;
For whi the matter were to longe   *Because*
To name the birdes and wright her songe.
Whereof, annon, the thithinges ther   *tidings*
Unto the quene sonne browght wer   *soon*
725 Withe many 'alas' and many a doubte,
Shewinge the shippes ther without.   *Announcing*
Tho can the aged lady weppe
And sayd, 'Allas, your joye on slepe   *joy to sleep*
Sone shal be browght; ye, long or night!
730 For we distroyed bene by this knyght.
For certes it may none other be
But he is of yened companie,   *yonder*
And thay be come him here to seche.'   *seek*
And withe that word her fayled speche.
735 'Witheout remedy we be distroyed,'
Full ofte sayd all, and con conclude,
Holy at once at the laste,
That best was shett ther yattes faste,   *to shut; gates*
And arme them all in good langauge,
740 As they had done of old usage,
And of fayre wordes make ther shoot.   *ammunition*
And this was ther counsell and the knot.   *main point*
And other purpose toke they none,
But, armed thus, forthe they gone
745 Towarde the walles of the Ile.
But or they come ther longe while,
They mette the great lord of above
That cauled is the God of Love   *called*
That hem advised withe suche chere   *looked at them*
750 Right as he withe them angrye were.
Avayled them not ther walles of glasse —
This mighty lord lett not to passe —   *was not hindered*
Ne shettinge of ther yattes fast.
All they had ordayned was but wast;   *a waste*
755 For when his shipe had founde londe,
This lord anone withe bowe in hande,
In to this Ile withe huge presse   *throng*

Hyed fast, and wold not ceasse   *Hastened*
Tyll he come where this knyght laye.
760   Of quene ne ladye by the waye
Toke he no hedd, but forthe past —   *heed*
And yet all followed at the laste.
And when he come where laye the knight,
Well shewed he he had great might,
765   And forthe the quene cauled, anone,
And all the ladyes everychone,
And to them sayde: 'Is this not rothe   *a pity*
To se my servaunte for his trothe
Thus lene, thus syke, and in this paine,
770   And wote not unto home to plaine,   *whom to complain*
Save onlye one, witheout mo,
Wiche might him helle and is his foo?'   *heal*
And withe that word, his hevye browe
He shewed the quene, and loked rowghe.   *fierce*
775   This mighty lord, forthe tho annone,
Withe o loke, her feautes echeon   *faults*
He can her shew in littell speche,   *in few words*
Comaundinge her to be his leche.   *physician*
Witheout more, shortlye to saye,
780   He thawght the quene sonne shuld obye.   *soon; obey*
And in his hannd he shoke his bowe,
And sayd right sone he wolde be know; *acknowledged as lord*
And for she had so longe refused
His servaunte, and his lawes not used,
785   He lett her witt that he was wrothe,   *let her know*
And bent his bowe, and forthe he goethe
A paace or two, and even here
A large drawght up to his eare
He drew, and withe an arrow ground *sharpened by grinding*
790   Sharpe and new, the quene a woounde
He gave that pearced unto the harte,
Wiche afterward full sore can smarte,
And was not holle of many a yere.   *healed for*
And even withe that: 'Be of good chere,
795   My knyght,' quod he. 'I will the hele,   *heal you*

89

And the restore to parfyte wele.   *well-being*
And for eche payne thou hast endured,
To have two joyes thou ar ewred.'   *happily destined*

And forthe he past by the rowte   *crowd*
800   Withe sobre chere, walkynge aboute,
And what he sayd I thowght to here.
Well wist he wiche his servauntes were,   *knew*
And as he passed, annone he found
My lady, and her toke by the hande,
805   And made her chere as a goddesse,
And of beutye he cauled her princesse;
Of bountye eke gave her the name,
And sayd ther was nothinge blame   *to be blamed*
In her but she was vertuus,
810   Savinge she wolde no pitye use,
Wiche was the cause he ther her sawght
To put that faute owt of her thawght.   *deficiency*
And sythe she had the hole riches
Of womanehed and frendlynes,
815   He sayd it was nothinge syttinge   *appropriate*
To voyd petye his owne lodginge;   *thrust out pity from*
And can her preache and withe her playe,   *converse lightly*
And of her beawtye tolde her aye,   *repeatedly*
And sayd she was a creature
820   Off whom the name shuld longe dewer   *endure*
And in bookes full of plesaunse
Be put for ever in remembraunce.
And as me thowght, more frindlyely
Unto my ladye and goodlelye
825   He spake, then any that was ther;
And for the apples, I trow yt were,
That she had in possession.
Wherefor longe in processyon,
Many a paace, arme under other,
830   He walked, and so did with none other.
But what he wold comaunde or saye
Forthewithe neades all must obeye;   *Straightway*

And what he desyred at the least
Of my ladye, was by requeste.
835 And when they longe together had bene,
He browght my ladye to the quene,
And to her sayd: 'So God you spede,
Shew grace, consentes, that is neade.'   *needful*
My ladye, tho, full conninglye,
840 Right well avised and womanlye,   *Very judicious*
Downe cone to knele uppon the flores,
Whiche Aprell nurrished had with showers,
And to this mightye lord cane saye,
'That pleassethe you, I woll obeye   *What*
845 And me restraine from other thowght;
As ye woll, all thinges shal be wrought.'
And withe that word, knelinge, she qwoke.
That mightye lord in armes her toke
And sayd: 'Ye have a sarvaunte, one
850 That trewer livinge is ther none;
Wherefore, god were, seinge his trothe,   *it were good*
That on his paynes ye had rothe   *compassion*
And purposed you to here his speche,
Fullye avised him to leche.   *resolved; cure*
855 For of one thinge ye may be suer: *certain*
He wil be youres while he may duer.'
And withe that word, right on his game,   *in his playful way*
Me thowght he lowghe and tolde my name,   *laughed*
Wiche was to me marvell and fere,
860 That what to do I nist there,   *did not know*
Ne whither me was better or none
Ther to abyde or thence to gone.
For well wend I my ladye wolde   *thought*
Imagen or deme that I had tolde
865 My counsell hole, or made complainte   *whole secret*
Unto that lorde, that mightye saynte;
So verelye eche thinge unsawght   *accurately; unasked*
He sayd as he had know my thought,   *known*
And tolde my trothe and myn unease
870 Bet then I couthe for myn ease,

91

Tho I had studied all a weake.   *a whole week*
Well wist that lord that I was syke
And wold be leched wonder faine.   *healed*
No mane me blame; myne was the paine.   *I blame no one*
875   And when this lord had all sayd
And longe withe my ladye playd,
She can to smyle withe sprite glade.
This was the answere that she mad,   *This (the smile)*
Wiche put me there in dowble paine,
880   That what to do, ne what to sayne,
Wist I not ne what was the best.
Fare was myn harte tho from his rest: *Far*
For as I thowght that smylinge sygne
Was token that the hart inclyne
885   Wold to request reasonable,
By cause smylinge is favorable
To every thinge that shall thrive,
So thowght I tho, anon belyve,   *So too; just as quickly*
That wordeles answere in no towne   *in no place*
890   Was tane for obligacyon,   *taken*
Ne cauled sewertye, in no wyse,   *certainty*
Amonges them that cauled bene wise.
Thus was I in a joyous doubte,
Suer an unsurest of that rowte.   *and*
895   Right as myn hart thowght it were,
So more or lesse woxe my fere,   *grew*
That yf one thowght made it well,
Annother shente yt everye deale,   *destroyed; every bit*
Till at the last I couthe no more,
900   But porposed, as I dyd before,
To serve trewelye my lyves space,   *the duration of my life*
Awaytinge ever the yere of grace
Wiche may fall yet or I sterve,   *befall; before I die*
Yf it please her that I serve,
905   And served have, and wil do ever.
For thinge is none that me is lever   *more precious*
Then her service, whose presence
Myn heven is hole, and her absence   *Is my whole heaven*

An hell full of diverse paines
910　Wiche to the deathe full oft me straynes.

Thus in my thowghtes, as I stode —
That unethe felt I harme ne good —　　　　　　　　*hardly*
I sawe the quene at littell paace　　　　　　　　*very slowly*
Come where this mightye lord was,
915　And kneled downe in presence there
Of all the ladyes that ther were,
Withe sobre countenance avised,　　　　　　　　*well-composed*
In fewe wordes that well sufficed,
And to this lord, annon, pressent
920　A byll, wherin hol her intente　　　　　　　　*letter; wholly*
Was writton, and how she besowght,
As he knew every will and thought,
That of his godhede and his grace　　　　　　　　*goodness*
He wold forgeve all old trespace,
925　And undispleased be of tyme past,
For she wold ever be stedfaste,
And, in his service, to the deathe
Use every thought wall she had breathe,　　　　　　*while*
And syght, and wepte, and sayde no more.　　　　　*sighed*
930　Withein was wrytton all the sore.
At wiche bill the lord cane smyle,
And sayd he wold withein that Ile
Be lord and syr, bothe est and west;　　　　　　　*sire*
And cauled it ther his new conquest,
935　And in great counsell toke the quene.
Longe were the tales them betwene.
And over her bill he rede thrise,
And wonder gladlye con devise　　　　　　　　　*gave an account of*
Her features fayer and hir visage,
940　And bad good thrifte on that image,　　　　　　*wished good success*
And sayd he trowed her complaynet
Shuld after cause her be corseint [1]
And in his sleve he put the bill —

---

[1] *Should afterward cause her to be [thought of as] a saint*

Was ther none that knewe his will —
945 And forthe walked apace abowte, *briskly*
Beholdinge all the lustye rowte, *pleasant company*
Halfe in a thowght, withe smylinge chere,
Till, at the last, as ye shall here,
He torned unto the quene agayne
950 And sayd: 'To morne, here in this playne *Tomorrow morning*
I woll ye be, and all yours
That purposed bene to were flowers
Or of my lustye collours use.
It may not be to you excuse, *There may*
955 Ne none of youres, in no wyse,
That able be to my service. *are capable*
For, as I sayd have here before,
I woll be lord for evermore
Of you, and of this Ile and all,
960 And of all youres that have shall
Joye, peace, or easse, or in pleasaunce
Your lives use witheoute mischaunce;
Here will I in estate be sene' — *in my position of power*
And turned his visage to the quene —
965 'And you geve knowledge of my will,
And a full answere of youre bill.'
Was ther non 'ney,' ne wordes none,
But very obeysaunt semed eche one, *obedient*
Quene and other that were there.
970 Well semed yt they had great feare.
And toke lodginge every wyght;
Was none departed of that night.
And some to reade old romansys
Hem occupied for ther pleasaunces,
975 Some to make virleyes and leyes, *virelays and lays*
And some to other diverse pleyes.
And I to me a romaunse toke,
And as I readinge was the booke,
Me thowght the spere had so rone *sphere; run*
980 That it was risinge of the sonne,
And suche a presse into the playne *crowd*

94

Assemble con, that withe great paine
One might for other go ne stande,   *because of others nearby*
Ne none take other by the hand
985   Witheouten they distorbed were,
So huge and great the presse was ther.

And after that, within two oweres,   *hours*
This mightye lord, all in flowers
Of diverse coloures many a payer,   *pair*
990   In his estate up in the eyer,
Well to fadome as his hight, [1]
He sett him ther in all ther syght;
And for the quene, and for the knyght,
And for my ladye, and every wyght
995   In hast he sende, so that never one   *sent*
Was ther absent, but come echeon.
And when thay thus assembled were,
As ye have hard me saye you here,   *heard*
Witheout more tarringe, on hight,
1000   Ther to be sene of everye wyght,
Up stood, amonge the presse above,
A counseler, servaunt of Love,
Wiche semed well of great estate;
And shewed ther how no debate   *argument [against God of Love]*
1005   Ofte ne goodlye might be used   *Ought nor properly might*
In gentullnes and be excussed.   *courtesy*
Wherefore he sayd his lordes will
Was, every wyght there shuld be still
And in peace and one accorde,
1010   And thus comaunded at a word.   *instantly*
And cane his tonge to suche laungauge
Turne, that yet in all his age   *in all of his age*
Hard I never so coninglye   *Heard*
Man speke, ne halfe so faythefullye;
1015   For every thinge he sayd there
Semed as it insealed were   *had the seal of authority*

---

[1] *Easily two fathoms (twelve feet) high*

95

Or appreved for very trew.   *confirmed; absolute truth*
Shuche was his conninge langauge new,   *Such*
And well accordinge to his chere,
1020   That, where I be, me thinke I here   *hear*
Him yet alwaye, when I my one   *on my own*
In any place may be allone.
First con he of the lustye Ile
All the astate in little while   *condition*
1025   Reherse, and hollye every thinge
That caused ther his lordes cominge;
And everye wele, and every wo,
And for what cause eche thinge was so,
Well shewed he there, in easye speche;   *unhurried*
1030   And how the syke had nede of leche,   *sick; physician*
And who that whole was and in grace,
He told playnelye how eche thinge was.
And, at the last, he con conclude,
Voydinge every language rude,   *Avoiding*
1035   And sayd that prince, that mightye lord,
Or his depertinge wold accorde   *Before his departure*
All the perties ther presente,
And was the fyne of his entente: *And that was; whole point*
'Wittnesse his presence in your syght
1040   Whiche syttes amonge you in his might.'
And kneled downe, witheowten more,
And no o word spoke he more.   *not a single word*

Tho can this mightye lord him dresse,   *prepared to rise*
Withe chere avised to do largesse, [1]
1045   And sayd unto this knyght and me:
'Ye shall to joye restored be.
And for ye have bene trewe, ye twayne,
I graunte you here for every payne
A thousand joyes everye weckee,   *week*
1050   And look ye be no lenger syke;   *no longer sick*
And bothe your ladyes — lo them here! —

---

[1] *By his manner resolved to be generous*

Take eche his owne. Beth of good chere!
Your happye daye is now begonne
Sythe yt was rissinge of the sunne.
1055 And to all other in this place,
I graunt hollye to staund in grace
That servethe trewelye witheout slowthe
And to avanced be, by trothe.'
Tho can this knyght and I downe knele,
1060 Weninge to do wonder well,   *Thinking*
Sayinge, 'O Lord, your great mercye
Us hathe enriched so openly,
That we deserve may nevermore
The least parte, but evermore
1065 Withe sowle and bodye trulye serve
You and yours till we sterve.'   *die*
And to oure ladyes, ther they stood,   *where*
This knyght that cothe so mikle good   *much*
Whent in hast, and I allso —
1070 Joyeux and glad were we tho,
And as riche in everye thowght
As he that all hathe and owe nowght —   *owes*
And them besoute, in humble wise,   *besought*
Us t'accepte to ther service
1075 And shewe us of ther frendlye cheres,
Wiche in ther treasure many yeres
They kepte had, us to great paine;   *to our great distress*
And told that servauntes twayne
Were, and wolde be, and so had ever,   *had [been]*
1080 And for the deathe chaunge wold we never,   *even in the face of death*
Ne do offence, ne thinge leke yll,   *nor anything like an injury*
But full ther ordinaunce and will;   *fulfill*
And made oure othes freshe new,
Oure olde servaunce to renewe,   *service*
1085 And hollye thers for evermore
We ther become, what might we more,   *whatever*
And well awaytinge that in slowghth   *watching out; sloth*

We made no faute, ne in no trothe, [1]
Ne thowght not do, I you ensure,   *Nor thought not to do [any]*
1090 Withe oure will while we may duer.

This season past, againse an eve   *time; towards one evening*
This lord of the quene toke leve,
And sayd he wold hastelye retorne
And at good leasure there sojorne,
1095 Bothe for his honor and her ease,
Comaundinge fast the knyght to please.   *Commanding [her] earnestly*
And gave his statutes in papers,
And ordayned diverse officers,
And forthe to shipe the same nyght
1100 He wente, and sone was owt of syght.
And on the morrow, when the ayere
Attempered was and wether fayer,   *More temperate*
Erlye at rysinge of the sonne,
After the nyght awaye was ronne,
1105 Playinge us on the rivage,   *Chatting playfully; shore*
My lady spake of her viage,   *journey*
And sayd she made smale jorneys   *was accustomed to make*
And held her in straunge conteryes;
And forthewithe to the quene went,
1110 And shewed her holly her entent,
And toke her leve withe chere wepinge,   *in a tearful manner*
That petye it was to se that partinge.
For to the quene it was a paine
As to a martyre new slayne;
1115 That for her woo, and she so tender,
Yet wepe I ofte, when I remembre.
She offered ther to resyne   *resign*
To my ladye, eyght tymes or nyne,
Th'astate, the Ile, shortlye to tell,
1120 If it might please her ther to dwell;
And sayd forever her linage   *kin*
Shuld to my lady do omage

---

[1] *We committed no fault, nor erred with regard to truth*

98

	And herrs be holl, witheowten more,	
	They and all thers for evermore.	
1125	'Naye, God forbyd,' my ladye ofte	
	Withe many connynge wordes and softe	*skillfully chosen*
	Sayd, 'that ever suche thinge shuld bene	
	That I consent shulde that a quene	
	Of youre estate, and so well named,	*and of such a high reputation*
1130	In any wise shuld be entamed!	*harmed*
	But wold be fayne withe all my hart,	
	What so befell or how me smarte,	*or however I was hurt*
	To do thinge that you might please	
	In any wise, or be your ease.'	
1135	And kysed ther, and bad goodnyght.	
	For wiche leve wepte many a wyght.	*leave-taking*
	Ther might men here my ladye preysed,	
	And suche a name of her arrayssed —	*exalted*
	What of connynge and fryndlyenes,	
1140	What of beautye withe jentulnes,	
	What of glad and frendlye cheres	
	That she used in all her yeres —	
	That wonder was here every wight	*to hear*
	To saye well how they did ther might.	*To speak well [of her]*
1145	And withe a prese, uppon the morrowe	
	To shipe her browght; and wich a sorrowe	*what*
	They made when she shuld under sayle,	*[begin to leave] under sail*
	That, and ye wyst, ye wold mervayle!	*if you knew*
	Forthe goethe the shipe; owt goethe the sonde;	*sounding-line*
1150	And I, as wood man unbownde,	*mad*
	For dowbte to be behinde there,	
	Into the see, witheowten feare,	
	Annone I ranne, till withe a wave	
	All sodenly I was overthrowghe;	
1155	And withe the water, to and fro,	
	Bacwarde and forward, traveled so,	*so battered*
	That mynd and brethe nyghe was gone,	
	That for good ne harme knew I none.	*I could not distinguish*
	Till, at the last, withe hockes twayne	*hooks*

1160	Men of the shipe withe mickle paine	
	To save my lyve dyd suche travell	*hard work*
	That, and ye wyst, ye wold mervell;	
	And in the shipe me drew on highe,	
	And sayden all that I wold dye,	
1165	And layd me longe downe by the maste,	*full length*
	And of ther clothes uppon me caste.	
	And ther I made my testament,	
	And wyst my selfe not what I mente;	
	But when I sayd had what I wolde,	
1170	And to the mast my wo all toulde,	
	And tane my leve at everye wight,	*taken*
	And closyd myn eyne, and lost my syght,	
	Avised to dye witheout more speche	*Resolved*
	Or any remedye to seche,	*seek*
1175	Of grace newe, as was grete ned,	
	My ladye of my paine toke hede,	
	And her bethought how that for trothe	*thought to herself*
	To se me dye it were great routhe;	
	And to me came in sobre wyse	
1180	And softelye sayd, 'I praye you, ryse.	
	Come on withe me; let be this fare.	*behavior*
	All shall be well. Have ye no care.	
	I woll obey, ye, and fulfyll	*yea*
	Holly in all that lordes will	
1185	That you and me, not longe ago,	
	After his liste comaunded so,	*desire*
	That ther agayne no resistaunce	
	May be, witheout great offence.	
	And therefore, here now what I saye.	
1190	I am, and wol be, frindlye aye.	
	Ryse up! Beholde this avauntage	*great favor*
	I graunt you in erytage,	*as a gift*
	Peaseble witheowt stryve	*strife*
	Duringe the dayes of your lyfe.'	
1195	And of her apples in my sleve	
	One she put, and toke her leve	
	In wordes few, and sayd, 'Good hele,	*health*

	He that all made you send, and wele!'	*well-being*
	Werewithe my paines, all at once,	
1200	Toke suche leve, that all my bones	
	For the newe ourewse pleasaunce,	*joyful*
	So as they cothe, desyred to daunce.	
	And I, as hole as any wyght,	
	Up rose withe joyoux harte and light,	
1205	Hole and unsyke, right well at ease,	
	And all forgett had my diseace;	
	And to my ladye, where she playd,	
	I went annone and to her sayd:	
	'He that all joyes, persones to plese,	
1210	First ordayned withe perfyt ease,	
	And everye pleasure cane departe,	*distributed*
	Send you, madame, as large parte;	*as large a part*
	And of his goodes suche plentye	
	As he has done you of bewtye,	
1215	Withe hele and all that maye be thowght,	
	He send you all, as he all wrought.	
	Madame,' quod I, 'Your servaunte trewe	
	Have I byne longe, and yet woll new,	*been; still will [be] anew*
	Witheowten chaunge or repentaunce	
1220	In any wise, or variaunce,	
	And so wool do, as thrive I ever;	*will*
	For thinge is none that me is lever	*dearer*
	Then you to please, however I fare,	
	Myn hartes ladye and my welfare,	
1225	My lyfe, myn hele, my leche also	
	Of every thinge that doth me wo,	
	Myn helpe at ned, and my suertye	*guarantee*
	Of everye joye that longes to me,	*belongs*
	My succors hole in all wyse	*My whole salvation*
1230	That may be thowght or man devise.	
	Your grace, madame, suche have I found	
	Now, in my nead, that I am bound	
	To you for ever, so Christ me save,	
	For hele and lyve of you I have;	*life*
1235	Wherefore is reason I you serve	

Withe dew obeysaunce till I starve,   *due obedience*
And so wil do by my trothe,'
Quod I, 'Madame, witheout slouthe,
And dead and quicke be ever youres,
1240   Late, erlye, and at all owers.'   *hours*
Tho can my ladye smyle a lyte,
And in playne englyshe on consyte,[1]
In wordes fewe, holl her entent
She shewed me ther, and how she ment
1245   To meward, in every wyse,   *Towards me*
Holly she can all ther devise
Witheout prosses or longe travell,[2]
Charginge me to kepe counsell   *the secret*
As I wold to her grace attayne;
1250   Of wiche comaundemente I was fayne.
Wherefore I passe over at this tyme,
For counsell cordes not well in ryme,[3]
And eak the othe, that I have swore,   *also*
To breke me were bet unbore;[4]
1255   Whi for untrewe for evermore   *The reason being that*
I shuld be hold, that nevermore
Of me in place shuld be reporte   *reported*
Thinge that avayle might or comfort
To mewardes in any wysse,   *Towards me; way*
1260   And eche wyght wold me dispice   *despise*
In that they couthe, and me repreve,   *Because of what they knew*
Whiche were a thinge sore for to greve;
Wherefore, hereof more mencyon
Make I not now, ne longe sermone,   *discourse*
1265   But shortlye thus I me excuse:
To ryme a counssell I refuce.

Saylinge thus, two dayes or thre,

---

[1] *And in plain English, according with her view of the matter*
[2] *Without a lot of words or laborious business*
[3] *For a secret is not appropriate to rhyme*
[4] *It were better for me not to have been born than to break it*

My ladye, towardes her cunterye,
Over the waves highe and grene
1270 Wiche were large and depe betwene,
Uppon a tyme me cauled, and sayd
That of my hele she was well paide;
And of the quene, and of the Ile,
She taled withe me longe while,   *talked*
1275 And of all that she there had sene,
And of th'astate, and of the quene,
And of the ladyes, name by name,
Two owres or mo, this was her game.   *hours; pleasure*
Till at the last the wynde can ryse,
1280 And blew so fast, and in suche wyse,
The shipe, that every wyght con saye:
'Madame, or eve be of this daye,   *before*
And God tofore, ye shal be there   *God willing*
As ye wold faynest that ye were;
1285 And doubte not that withein six owres
Ye shal be ther as all is youres.'   *there where*
At whiche wordes she cane to smyle,
And sayd that was no longe while
That they hur sett, and up she rosse,
1290 And all abowt the shipe she goes,
And mad good chere to everye wyght,
Till of the londe she had syght;
Of wiche syght glad, God yt wote,
She was, and abasshed annon a boote   *had a boat lowered at once*
1295 And forthe goethe, shortlye you to tell,
Where she accostomed was to dwell,
And recyved was, as good right,   *as was proper*
Withe joyeux chere and hartes light,
And as a glad newe aventure,   *a piece of good fortune*
1300 Pleasaunte to every creature.

Withe whiche landinge tho I woke,
And found my chaumbre full of smoke,
My chekes eke, unto the eares,   *cheeks*
And all my body weate of teares;   *wet*

1305	And all so feble and in suche wise	
	I was, that unethe might I rise,	*hardly*
	So fare traveled and so feynte,	*So greatly over-exerted*
	That neither knew I kyrk ne saynt,	*church*
	Ne what was what, ne who was who,	
1310	N'avysed what wey I wolde goo.	*Nor knew*
	But, by aventures grace,	*fortune's grace*
	I ryse and welke sawght paace and pace,	*walked soft step by step*
	Till I a windinge stayer founde,	*stair*
	And held the vice ay in my hand,	*central newel-shaft*
1315	And upwardes sauftelye so can crepe	*softly*
	Till I cam where I thowght to slepe	
	More at myn ease and owt of presse,	*out of danger*
	At my good leysure and in peace,	
	Till somewhat I recoumfort were	
1320	Of the travell and great feare	
	That I indured had before:	
	This was my thought, witheowt more.	
	And as a wyght wittles and faynte,	
	Witheout more, in a chaumbre painte	
1325	Full of storyes old and diverse —	
	More then I cane now reherse —	
	Unto a bed full soberlye,	*[I approached] a bed*
	So as I might full sauftelye,	*softly*
	Pace after other, and nothinge sayd.	*Step by step*
1330	Till, at the last, downe I me layde;	
	And, as my mynd wolde geve me leve,	
	All that I dremed had that eve	
	Before, all I con reherse,	
	Right as a childe at skole his vearse	
1335	Dothe, after that he thinkethe to thrive,	*in so far as he*
	Right so did I; for all my lyve	
	I thawght to have in remembraunce —	
	Bothe the paine and the pleasaunce —	
	The dreame, hole as yt me befell,	
1340	Wiche was as ye here me tell.	

Thus in my thowghtes as I laye,

That happy or unhappy daye —
Woote I not, so have I blame,   *even though I am to be blamed*
Of the two wiche is the name —
1345   Befell me so that ther a thought
By processe new on slepe me browght,   *In due course again*
And me governed so, in a while,
That agayne withein the Ile
Me thawght I was; where of the knyght,
1350   And of the ladyes I had a syght,
And were assembled on a grene,
Knyght and lady withe the quene;
At wiche assemble ther was sayd
How they all content and payd   *pleased*
1355   Were holly, as in that o thinge,
That the knyght ther shuld be kynge,
And thay wold all for suer wytnes
Wedded be, bothe more and lesse,[1]
In remembraunce, witheout more;
1360   Thus they concente for evermore.
And was concluded that the knyght
Departe shulde the same nyght,
And forthewithe ther take his viage,
To jorneye for his mariage
1365   And retorne withe suche an ooste   *a host*
That weddid might be lest and most;   *the least and the greatest*
This was concluded, writton, and sealed,
That yt might not be repeled
In no wyse, but aye be fyrme,
1370   And all shuld be withein a terme   *a set time*
Witheouwt more excusacyon,
Bothe feast and coronacyon.

This knyght, wiche had thereof the charge,
Annone into a littull barge
1375   Browght was, late ageynst an eve,   *late towards one evening*
Where of all he toke his leave;

---

[1] *Wedded be, both those of higher and those of lower rank*

	Wiche barge was a manes thowght,
	After his pleasure it him browght;
	The quene herselfe accostomed aye
1380	In the same barge to pleye.
	Yt nedethe nether mast ne rother —
	I have not hard of suche another —
	Ne master for the governaunce;
	Hit sayled by thowght and by pleasaunce,
1385	Witheowt labor, est or west
	All was one, calme and tempest.
	And I wente withe, at his requeste,
	And was the first prayed to the fest.
	When he come in his cuntrye,
1390	And passed had the wavy sea,
	In an haven, depe and large,
	He left his riche and noble barge,
	And to the court, shortlye to tell,
	He wente, where he was wont to dwell;
1395	And was receyved as good right
	As heyre and for a worthi knyght,
	Withe all the stattes of the lande
	Wiche come annon at his first sende,
	Withe glad spirites, full of trothe,
1400	Lothe to do faute, or withe a slouthe
	Attaynte be in any wyse —
	Ther riches was ther olde service,
	Wiche ever trew had be founde
	Sythe first inhabyte was the lond.
1405	And so receyved ther there kynge,
	That forgotten was nothinge
	That owe to be done, ne might please,
	Ne ther soverayne lord do ease,
	And withe them so, shortlye to saye,
1410	As they of custome had done aye.
	For seven yere past was, and more,
	The father, the olde, wyse and hoore
	Kinge of the lande, toke his leve
	Of all his barones one an eve,

Glosses (right margin):

- 1381 *rudder*
- 1382 *heard*
- 1387 *with [him]*
- 1388 *invited*
- 1395 *as was proper*
- 1397 *persons of rank*
- 1398 *summons*
- 1401 *Be found guilty*
- 1407 *ought*
- 1409 *And [done] by them thus*
- 1411 *For it was seven years ago*
- 1412 *[Since] the father; grey-haired*

1415 And tolde them how his dayes past
Were all, and comen was the laste;
And hartelye prayd hem to remembre,
His sonne, wiche yonge was and tender,
That borne was ther prince to be,
1420 Yf he retorne to that cuntrye
Might, be aventure or grace,   *by good fortune*
Withein any tyme or space;
And to be trewe and frindlye aye,
As they to him had bene allweye,
1425 Thus he them prayd, witheowt more,
And toke his leve for evermore.
Knowne was how, in tender age
This younge prince a great viage,
Oncouthe and straunge, onors to sekche,   *Marvellous; honors; seek*
1430 Toke on hand, withe littull speche;
Wiche was to seke a princes   *princess*
That he desyred more then riches
For her great name that flowred so,
That in that tyme ther was no moo
1435 Of her estate, ne so well named,   *rank; spoken of*
For borne was none that ever hir blamed;
Of wiche princes, sumewhat before
Here have I spoke, and sonne will more.   *soon*

So thus befell as ye shall here.
1440 Unto the lord they made suche chere,
That joye was, there to be presente
To se ther trothe and how they ment;
So very glade they were echeone,
That them amonge ther was not one
1445 That desyred more riches
Than for ther lord suche a princes,
That they might please and that were fayer;
For faste desyred they an heyer,   *heir*
And sayd great suertye were, iwis. [1]

---

[1] *And said it would be a source of great security, truly*

1450	And as they were speakinge of this,	
	The prince himeselfe him avised,	*made up his mind*
	And in playne englyshe undisgised	
	Them shewed hole his jorneye,	
	And of ther counsell can them praye;	
1455	And tolde how he ensured was,	*committed*
	And how his daye he might not passe	*due date*
	Witheouwt dishonor and great blame	
	And to him forever a shame;	
	And of ther counsell and avise	
1460	There he prayed them, once or twyse,	
	And that they wolde withein ten dayes	
	Avise and ordayne him suche wayes	*Advise*
	So that it were no displeasaunce,	
	Ne to this reme over great grevaunce,	*realm; excessive*
1465	And that he have might to his feaste	
	Sixti thousannd at the leaste;	
	For his intente withein short while	
	Was to retorne unto this Ile	
	That he came fro, and kepe his daye:	
1470	For nothinge wolde he be awaye.	*Not for anything*
	To counsell tho the lordes annone	
	Into a chaumbre everychon	
	Together went, them to devyse	
	How they might best, and in what wise,	
1475	Purveye for ther lordes pleasaunce	
	And the realmes contynuaunce	
	Of honor, whiche in it before	
	Had contynewed evermore.	
	So, at the last, they founde the weys	
1480	How withein the next fyftene dayes	
	All myght withe paine and diligence	
	Be done, and cast what the dispence	*estimated; expense*
	Might draw and, in conclusyon,	*amount to*
	Made for eache thinge provisyon.	
1485	When this was done hollye, tofore	
	The prince, the lordes all before	

Come and shewed what they had done,
And how they couthe by no reason
Fynde that within the ten dayes
1490 He myght departe, by no wayes,
But wolde be fiftene at least
Or he retorne might to his feaste;
And shewed him every reason whi
Yt myght not be so hastelye
1495 As he desyred, ne his daye
He might not kepe by no waye,
For diverse causes wonder greate.
Wiche when he hard, in suche a heate
He fell for sorrowe, and was syke
1500 Stil in his bed hole that weake   *all that week*
And nyghe the tother, for the shame,   *And most of the next*
And for the dowbte, and for the blame
That might on him be arette.   *attributed*
And oft uppon his brest he bette,
1505 And sayd: 'Allas! Myn honor for aye
Have I here lost clene this daye.
Ded wold I be! Allas, my name   *I wish I were dead*
Shall aye be more henseforthe in shame,   *Shall be for evermore*
And I disonered and repreved   *reproved*
1510 And never more shal be beleved!'
And made suche sorowe that, in trothe,
Him to behold it was great rothe.

And so endured the dayes fyftene
Till that the lordes, of an even,   *one evening*
1515 Him come and toulde they reydye wayre,   *were ready*
And shewed, in fewe wordes there,
How and what wysse they had purveyd   *in what way*
For his estate; unto him sayde
That twentye thousannd knyghtes of name
1520 And fortye thousande witheowt blame,
All come of noble lyne,
Togather in a companye
Were lodged on a ryvers syde,

Him and his pleasures ther to abyde.
1525 The prince, tho, for joye uprosse
And, were they lodged were, he goes, *And, where*
Witheout more, the same nyght,
And ther his supper made to dytte, *caused to be prepared*
And withe them boode till it was daye, *remained*
1530 And forthewithe so toke his jorneye,
Levinge the streyght, holdinge the large,[1]
Till he come till his noble barge. *to*
And when this prince, this lusty knyght,
Withe his pepull in armes bright
1535 Was comen where he thowght to passe, *embark*
And knewe well none abyden was
Behind, but all were there present,
Forthewithe annone all his entent
He told them ther, and made his cryes *proclamations*
1540 Throwghe his host that daye twyse,
Comandinge every lyves wight, *living creature*
Ther beinge present in his syght,
To be the morrowe on the rivage *shore*
Where he begine wold his vioage.
1545 The morrow come; the crye was kept; *the proclamation was kept*
Fewe was ther that night that slepte,
But trussed and purveyed for the morowe. *packed and provided*
Faute of shippes was all ther sorrowe; *Lack*
For save the barge and other two,
1550 Of shippes ther sawe I no moe.
Thus in ther dowbtes as they stode,
Waxinge the see, cominge the flode, *The sea rising, the tide coming in*
Was cryed: 'To shipe go, everye wight!'
Then was but hye that hye myght. *everyone hurrying that could*
1555 Unto the barge, me thowght, echeon
They wente; witheout was lefte not one — *outside*
Horse, male, trusse, ne baggage, *bag, package*
Sallett, spere, gardbrace, ne page — *Helmet; arm-guard*
But was loudged and rome inowghe.

---

[1] *Leaving the narrow [path], keeping to the broad [highway]*

110

1560	At wiche shippinge me thought I lowghe,	*feat of ship-loading; laughed*
	And cane to marvell in my thought	
	How ever suche a shipe was wrought;	
	For what people that cane increasse	*whatever the number of people*
	Ne never so thicke might be the presse,	*And however thick*
1565	But all had rome at ther will.	*room*
	Ther was not one that was lodged yll;	
	For, as I trow, my selfe the laste	
	Was one that lodged by the mast,	
	And where I loked I sawe suche rome	
1570	As all were lodged in a towne.	

	Forthe goethe the shipe; sayd was the crede;	
	And on ther knees, for ther good spedde,	*good success*
	Downe kneled everye wight a while	
	And prayed fast unto the Ile	*prayed [that]*
1575	They might come in savetye,	*safety*
	The prince and all the companye,	
	Withe worshipe and witheout blame	
	Or disslaunder of his name	
	Of the promese he shuld retorne	*Concerning the promise*
1580	Withein the tyme he did sojorne	
	In his land, biddinge his hoost —	*summoning his retinue*
	This was ther prayer, lest and most.	
	To kepe the daye duye, it might not bene,	*due*
	That he appoynt had withe the quene,	
1585	To retorne witheowt slouthe,	
	And so assured had his trothe.	
	For wiche faute, this prince, this knygkte,	
	Durynge the tyme slepte not a night;	
	Suche was his woo and his disease,	
1590	For dowbt he shuld the quene displeace.	

	Forthe goethe the shipe withe suche spede,	
	Right as the prince for his great neade	
	Desyer wolde after his thawghte,	
	Till it unto the Ile him browght;	
1595	Were in hast, upon the sannde,	*Where; beach*

111

He and his people toke the land   *disembarked*
Withe hartes glade and chere light,
Weninge to be in heven that night.   *Thinking*
But or they passed had a myle,
1600   Enteringe in toward that Ile,
All cladd in blacke withe chere peteus
A lady, wiche never dispeteouse   *cruel*
Had be in all her lyfe tofore,
Withe sorye chere and harte to-tore,   *torn to pieces*
1605   Unto this prince, where he cane ryde,
Come and sayde: 'Abyde! Abyde!
And have no hast, but fast retorne.   *instantly*
No reason is ye here sojorne,
For your untrothe hathe us distroyed;
1610   Woo worthe the tyme we us alyed   *Woe be to*
Withe you, that ar so sone untrewe.
Allas the daye that we you knewe!
Allas the tyme that ye were bore;   *born*
For all this land by you is lore!   *lost*
1615   Accursed be he you hether browght,
For all oure joye is turned to nowght.
Youre accquayntaunce we may complayne,
Wiche is the cause of all oure peine.'
'Allas, madame!' quod tho this knight;
1620   And withe that from his horse he light
Withe color pale and chekes lene.
'Allas, what is this for to mene?
What have ye sayde? Whi be you wrothe?
You to displease I wold be lothe.
1625   Knowe ye not well the promese
I made have to youre princes,
Wiche to performe is myne entent,
So mote I sped, as I have mente,   *So may I prosper*
And as I am her verye trewe,   *very true [servant]*
1630   Witheowte chaunge or thowght new,
And also solelye her seruaunte   *solely*
As creature or man lyvenante   *living*
May be to ladye or princes;

For she myn heven and hole riches
1635   Is, and the ladye of myn hele,
My wordes joye and all my wele.   *world's*
What maye this be? Wense comes this speche?   *Whence*
Tell me, madame, I you beseche;
For sythe the first of my lyvinge   *the first day of my life*
1640   Was I so fearfull of nothinge
As I am now to here you speke.
For dowbte I feale my harte brecke.
Say on, madame! Tell me your will.
The remenaunt is it good or ill?'

1645   'Allas,' quod she, 'that you ware bore!
For, for your love, this land is lore;
The quene is ded, and that is rothe,   *pity*
For sorrow of your great untrothe.
Of two partes of the lusty rowte   *Some two thirds*
1650   Of ladyes that were here abowte,
That wonte were to tale and pleye,   *chat*
Nowe ar ded and clene awaye,
And under earthe tane lodginge newe.   *taken*
Alas, that ever ye were untrewe!
1655   For when the tyme ye sett was paste,
The quene to counsell sone in hast —   *soon [went]*
What was to do? — and sayd great blame
Your accquayntaunce cause wold and shame,
And the ladyes of ther avise   *for their advice*
1660   Prayed, for nead was to be wisse   *need; wise*
In eschewinge tales and songes,
That by them make culd evell tunges,   *concerning them; could*
And say they were lyghtlye conquest   *easily conquered*
And prayed to a poore feast   *invited*
1665   And fowle had ther worshipe wayved,   *honor given up*
When so onwyselye they conceyved   *unwisely; thought*
Ther riche treasure and ther hele,   *happiness*
Ther famous name and ther wele,
To put in suche an aventure;   *to such hazard*
1670   Of wiche the slaunder ever duer   *ever to last*

	Was lyke, witheowt helpe of apele;	*appeal*
	Wherefore they nede had of counscell,	
	For everye wight of them wold saye	
	Ther closed Ile an open weye	
1675	Was become to every wight,	
	And well approved by a knyght,	*confirmed*
	Wiche he holles, witheowt pesaunce,	*entirely; trouble*
	Had sone atcheved th'obeysaunce.	
	All this was meved at counsell thrise,	*put forward for discussion*
1680	And concludedd daylye twise,	
	That bet was dye witheowt blame	*it was better to die*
	Then losse the riches of her name.	*lose*
	Wherefor, the deathes acquantaunce	
	They chese, and leste have ther pleasaunce,	*chose; lost*
1685	For dowbte to lyve as repreved	*under reproof*
	In that they you so sone beleved;	
	And made ther othes withe one accord,	
	That eate, ne drinke, ne speke a worde	
	They shuld never, but ever wepinge	
1690	Byde in oo place witheout partinge,	
	And use ther dayes in penaunce,	
	Witheowt desyer of allegiaunce.	*alleviation*
	Of wiche the trothe annone con preve;	*was demonstrated*
	For whi the quene, forthewithe, her leve	*Because*
1695	Tooke at them all that were present,	
	Of her defautes fullye repente,	*repentant*
	And dyed there witheowten more.	
	Thus ar we lost for evermore.	
	What shuld I more hereof reherse?	
1700	Come on withe me. Come se the herse,	
	Where ye shall se the petiust syght	*most pitiful*
	That ever yet was shewed to knyght;	
	For ye shal se ladyes stand,	
	Eche withe a great rood in hand,	*rod*
1705	Clade in blacke, withe visage whight,	*white*
	Be rydye eche other for to smyte;	*ready*
	Yf any be that will not wepe,	
	Or who that makes countenaunce to slepe,	

114

	They be so bet, that also blewe	*beaten*
1710	They be, as clothe that dyed is newe.	
	Suche is ther perfyte repentaunce.	
	And thus they kepe ther ordinaunce,	
	And woll do ever to the deathe,	
	While them induers any brethe.'	
1715	This knyght, tho, in armes twayne	
	This ladye toke, and cone her saynne:	
	'Allas my birthe! Wo worthe my lyfe!'	*Woe is*
	And even withe that he drewe a knyfe	
	And thorowghe gowne, dublet, and shirte,	
1720	He made the blode cume from his hart;	
	And sett him downe uppon the grene,	
	And full repent, and closeyd his eyne,	*fully repented*
	And, save that once he drew his brethe,	
	Witheowt more thus he tooke his deathe.	
1725	For wiche cause, the lustye hoost	
	Whiche, in a battayle on the coste,[1]	
	At once, for sorrowe, suche a crye	
	Con reare thorowe the companye,	*Was raised*
	That to the heven hard was the sowne	*heard; noise*
1730	And under th' earthe as far downe,	
	That wild beastes for feare	
	So sodanlye aferde awere,	
	That for the doubt, while they might duer,	
	They ranne as of ther lyves unsuer	
1735	From the woddes untto the plaine,	
	And from the valles the highe mountayne	
	They sowght, and rane as bestes blind	
	That clene forgetten had ther kynd.	*nature*
	This wo not ceassed, to counsell went	
1740	This lordes, and for that ladye sente,	
	And of avise what was to done	*advice; to be done*
	They her besowght she saye wold sone.	

---

[1] *Which [was still] in battle-formation on the coast*

115

Wepinge full sore, all clad in blacke,
This ladye saftelye to them spake,   *softly*
1745   And sayd: 'My lordes, by my trothe,
This mischeve holl is of your slouthe.   *whole; due to your*
And yf ye had, that judge wold right,   *[you] that would judge rightly*
A prince that were a very knyght,   *a true*
Ye that bene of estate, eche one
1750   Dye for his faute shulde, one and one;   *one by one*
For ye hold had the promesse,   *if you had kept*
And done that longes to jentulnes,   *belongs*
And fulfilled the prince behest,
This hastye harme had bene a feast,   *sudden; celebration*
1755   And now is unrecoverable,
And us a slaunder aye durable.   *to us; lasting forever*
Wherefore I saye, as of counsell,
In me is none that may avayle;
But, yf you list, for remembraunce,   *if it pleases you*
1760   Purveye and make such ordinaunce
That the quene, that was so meke,
Withe all her wemen, ded or syke,
Might in your land a chapell have,
Withe some remembraunce on her grave
1765   Shewinge her end withe the petye,   *all piteous circumstances*
In somme notable olde cetye,   *city*
Nighe unto an highe-waye
Where everye wight might for her praye,
And for all heres that have bene trewe.'   *hers (i.e., women)*
1770   And even withe that she chaunged hewe,
And twise wished after the deathe,
And syght, and thus passed her brethe.   *sighed*

Then sayd the lordes of the ooste,
And so concluded lest and most,
1775   That they wold ever in houses of thacke   *thatch*
Ther lyves use, and were but blacke,   *spend; wear*
And forsake all ther pleasaunces,
And turne all joye to penaunces,
And bare the ded prince to the barge,   *And they bore*

116

1780 And named them shuld have the charge.	*appointed those who*
And to the hearse where laye the quene	
The remenante went, and downe on knene,	
Holdinge ther handes on hight, con crye,	
'Mercy! Mercy!' everiche thrye;	*each one thrice*
1785 And cursed the tyme that ever slouthe	
Shuld have suche masterdome of trothe.	
And to the barge, a long mile,	
They bere her forthe, and in a while	
All the ladyes, one and one,	
1790 By companies were browght echeon;	
And past the see, and toke the lande,	*crossed over; landed*
And in newe hersses on a sannde	*hearses; beach*
Put, and browght were all annone	
Unto a cety clossed withe stone,	
1795 Where it had bene used aye	*been ever the custom*
The kynges of the lannd to leye	
After they reyned in honors,	
And wright was wiche were conquerers,	*And it was written*
In an abbye of nonnes wiche were blacke,	
1800 Wiche accostomed were to wacke,	*keep vigil*
And of ussage rysse eche a night	
To pray for everye lyves wight.	*living creature*
And as befell, as is the gyse,	*And so it befell; custom*
Ordayned and sayd was the service	
1805 Of the prince and of the quene	
As devoutlye as might bene;	
And after that, abowght the hercesse,	*about; hearses*
Many orrysonnes and vearses,	*prayers; verses*
Witheowt note, full softelye	*music*
1810 Sayd were and full hartelye,	*devoutly*
That all the night, till it was daye,	
The peple in the churche cone preye	
Unto the Hollye Trynite	*Holy*
Of those sowles to have petye.	
1815 And when the night past and ronne	
Was, and the newe daye begonne,	

The yonge morrowe withe rayes redd,
Wiche from the sonne over all con spredd,
Attempered cleare was and fayer,   *Was made mild and clear*
1820   And made a tyme of holsome ayer,   *air*
Befell a wonder case and straunge   *an astonishing happening*
Amonge the people, and con chaunge
Sone the worde and everye woo   *the decree of destiny*
Unto a joye, and some to two.
1825   A byrde all fethered blewe and grene,
Withe bright arrayes, lyke gold, betwene,   *streaks*
As smale thredes over every joynte,
All full of collors straunge and cointe,   *exotically beautiful*
Uncothe and wonderfull to syghte,   *Unfamiliar*
1830   Uppon the quenes herse cone lyghte,   *alighted*
And songe full lowe and softelye
Thre songes in his armoneye,
Unletted of every wight;   *Unhindered*
Till, at the last, an aged knyght,
1835   Whiche semed a man in great thought
Lyke as he sett all thinge at nawght,
Withe visage and eyne over-wepte,   *exhausted with weeping*
And pale as mane longe unslepte,
By the hersses as he stoode,
1840   Withe hasty handelinge of his hood   *touching [or doffing]*
Unto a prince that by him past,
Made the birde somewhat agast;   *frightened*
Wherefore he rose, and lefte his songe,
And departe from us amonge,
1845   And spred his winges for to passe
By the place he entered was;
And in his hast, shortlye to tell,
He him hurte, that bacwarde downe he fell
From a windowe, richelye painte
1850   Withe lyves of many a dyverse saynte,
And beate his winges, and bled faste,
And of the hurte thus dyed and paste,   *passed away*
And ley ther well an hower or more,
Till, at the last, of birdes a skore

1855	Come, and sembled at the place	*gathered*
	Where the windowe broken was,	
	And made suche weymentacyon,	*lamentation*
	That petye was to here the son	*sound*
	And the werbelinge of ther throtes	
1860	And the complainte in ther nottes,	
	Wiche from joye clene was reversed.	
	And of them on the glasse sone percsyd,	*one of them; pierced*
	And in his beke, of colours nyne,	
	An erb he browght, flowerles, all grene,	
1865	Full of smale leves and plaine,	
	Swerte, and longe, withe many a vayne;	*Dark*
	And where his fellowe laye thus ded,	
	This erbe downe layd by his hede,	
	And dressed hit full softelye,	*arranged*
1870	And hange his hede, and stode therbye.	
	Whiche erbe, in lesse then halfe an owere,	*hour*
	Cone over all knote, and after flower	*Burst into bud all over*
	Full owt, and rype the seade;	
	And right this one another feede	*And just as one [bird]*
1875	Wold, in his beake, he toke a grayne	
	And in his fellowes beke, certayne,	
	Yt put; and thus wethein the thirde,	*in a trice*
	Up stode and pruned him the birde	*preened*
	Wiche dede had be in all oure syght,	*dead*
1880	And bothe together forthe ther flyght	
	Toke, singinge, from us, and ther leve;	
	Was none disturbe them wold, ne greve.	
	And when they perted were and gone,	*departed*
	Th' abbas the seades sone echeon	*abbess*
1885	Gathered had, and in her hande	
	Th' erbe she helde, well avisaunte	*closely inspecting*
	The lefe, the sede, the stalke, the flower,	
	And sayd it had a good savor	
	And was no comone herbe to fynde	
1890	And well approved of uncothe kynde,	*confirmed; unfamiliar*
	And then other more vertuus;	

Who so yt have myght, for to use
In his neade — flower, lefe, or graine —
Of ther hele myght be certainge;
1895 And layd it downe uppon the hersse
Where lay the quene, and con rehersse
Eche one to other that they had sene.   *what*
And talinge this, the seade wox grene,   *And as they talked thus*
And on the drye herse con springe,
1900 Wiche me thowght a wonder thinge,
And after that, flower an new seade,   *[came] flower and*
Of wiche the pepull all toke hede
And sayd yt was some great miracle
Or medicyne more fyne then treacle,[1]
1905 And were well done ther to assaye   *And it would do well*
Yf yt might ease in any waye
The corsses wiche withe torche-lyght   *corpses*
Thay waked had ther, all that night.   *had kept vigil over*

Sone were the lordes there concent,   *consented*
1910 And all the pepull therto content,
Withe easye wordes and lyttull fare,   *little fuss*
And made the quenes visage bare,
Wiche shewed was to all abowte;
Wherefore in sowne fell hole the rowte,   *swoon; all the company*
1915 And were so sorye, most and leste,
That longe of wepinge they not ceased;   *for a long time*
For, of ther lord the remembraunce
Unto them was suche displeasaunce,
That for to lyve they cauled paine,   *they called living a pain*
1920 So were they verye trewe and playne.   *faithful and honest*
And after this, the good abbas
Of the greynes con chesse and dresse   *choose and prepare*
Thre, withe her fingers clene and smale;
And in the quenes mothe, be tall,   *mouth, consecutively*
1925 One after other full easelye
She put and full coninglye,

---

[1] *Or medicine more potent than any antidote [for poison]*

	Wiche sheewed sone suche vertu,	
	That preved was the medicyne trewe;	
	For withe a smylinge countenaunce	
1930	The quene uprose, and of usaunce,	*according to custom*
	As she was wonte, to everye wight	
	She made good chere; for wiche syght,	
	The people knelynge on the stones	
	Thowght they in heven were, sowle and bones.	
1935	Unto the prince where he laye	
	They went, to make the same assaye.	*attempt*
	And when the quene it understode,	
	And how the medicyne was good,	
	She prayed she might have the greynes	
1940	To releve him from the paines	
	Whiche she and he had bothe endured;	
	And to him wente, and so him ured,	*brought a happy destiny*
	That withein a lyttull space	
	Lustye and freshe one lyve he was,	*alive*
1945	And in good hele, and hole of speche,	*perfectly able to speak*
	And lowghe, and sayd, 'Gramercy, leche.'	*laughed; Many thanks*
	For whiche the joye throwgheowt the towne	
	So great was, that the belles sowne	
	Affrayde the peopull a jorneye [1]	
1950	Abowte the cetye everye waye	
	And comen and asked cause and whi	
	They rongen were so stattelelye.	*grandly*
	And after that, the quene, th' abbas,	
	Made dilligence, or theye wolde cease,	*Made every effort, before*
1955	Suche that of ladyes sonne a rowte	
	Suinge the quene was all abowte;	*Attending upon*
	And cauled by name eche one and tolde,	*counted them off*
	Was none forgotton, yonge ne olde.	
	There mighte mene se joyes newe,	*men*
1960	When the medicyne, fyne and trewe,	
	Thus restored had every wight,	
	As well the ladyes as the knyght,	

---

[1] *Frightened people the distance of a day's journey away*

121

Unto perfyte joye and hele,
That flyttinge they were in suche wele,   *abounding*
1965 As folke that wolde in no wyse
Desyer more perfyte parradysse.

And thus, when passed was the sorrowe,
Withe mickell joye, sone on the morrowe,
The kinge, the quene, and everye lord,
1970 Withe all the ladyes, by one accorde
A generall assemble
Gert crye thorowghe the cunterye;   *Caused to be proclaimed*
The whiche after, as ther intente,
Was turned to a parlament,
1975 Where was ordayned and avised   *resolved*
Everye thinge and devised   *worked out*
That please might to most and lest.   *everyone, regardless of rank*
And ther concluded was, the feast
Withein the Ile to be holde,
1980 Withe full concente of yonge and olde;
In the same wyse as before
All thinges shulde be, witheowten more;   *without more ado*
And shipeden, and thether went.   *[they] took ship*
And into straunge remes sent   *far-off realms*
1985 To kinges, quenes, and ducheces,
To diverse princes and princesses
Of ther linage, and cane praye,
Yf yt lyke them, at that daye
Of marriage, for ther sporte,
1990 Come se the Ile and them disporte,
Where shulde be justes and turneyes,
And armes done in other wayes,   *feats of arms*
Signifyinge over all the daye,   *Announcing everywhere*
After Aprell withein Maye.   *[Which should be] after*
1995 And was avised that ladyes twayne   *[it] was resolved*
Of good estate and wel besene,   *well turned out*
Withe certayne knightes and squiers,
And of the quenes officers,
In maner of imbassad   *embassy*

122

2000	Withe certeyne leters, closed and made,	*sealed*
	Shuld take the barge, and departe,	
	And seke my ladye evrye parte	
	Till they her founde, for any thinge;	*without fail*
	Bothe charged thus, quene and kinge,	
2005	And as ther ladye and misteris,	*as [she was]; mistress*
	For to beseke, of jentulnes,	
	At the daye ther for to bene.	
	And ofte her recomaunde the quene,	*commended herself [to her]*
	And prayed, for all loves, to hast;	
2010	For but she come, all woll be wast,	
	And the feast a busynes	*tedious chore*
	Witheout joye or lustynes;	
	And toke them tokenes, and god spede[1]	
	Prayed God send, after ther neade.	*according to*
2015	Forthe wente the ladyes and the knightes,	
	And were owt fourteen dayes and nightes,	
	And browght my ladye in ther barge,	
	And had well sped, and done the charge.	*commission*
	Whereof the quene so hartelye glad	
2020	Was, that in sothe shuche joyes she hadd	*such*
	When the shipe approched lannde,	
	That she my ladye on the sannde	
	Met, and in armes so constrayne,	*embraced*
	That wonder was beholde them twayne	
2025	Whiche, to my dome, duringe twelve oures,	*in my opinion; hours*
	Nether for heat ne watery showers	
	Departed not; ne companye,	*Did not separate*
	Savinge themselfe, bode none them bye,	*remained*
	But gave them leaysure, at ther ease,	
2030	To reherse joye and diseace,	*distress*
	After the pleasure and corrages	*stirrings of the spirit*
	Of ther yonge and tender ages;	
	And after, withe many a knyght	
	Browght were where, as for that nyght,	*[They] were brought*

---

[1] *And gave them tokens [of authentication] and good success*

2035	They parted not, for to pleasaunce	
	Consent was hart and countenaunce,	
	Bothe of the quene and my mistris:	
	This was that night ther busynes.	
	And one the morrowe, withe huge route —	
2040	This prince — of lordes him abowte,	
	Come, and to my ladye sayd	
	That of her cominge glad and well appaide	*pleased*
	He was, and full conninglye	
	Her thannked and full hertelye,	
2045	And lowghe, and smyled, and sayd, 'Iwis,	
	That was in dowbte in suerty es.'	*What; is now assured*
	And comaunde do dilygence,[1]	
	And spare for neyther golde ne spence,	*expense*
	But make redye; for, one the morrowe,	
2050	Weddid withe 'Seynt John to borowe'	*May St. John be my security*
	He wold be, witheouten more;	
	And let them wytt them, lesse and more.[2]	
	The morowe come, and the service	
	Of marriage in suche wyse	
2055	Sayd was, that with more honor	
	Was never prince ne connqueror	
	Wedd, ne withe suche companye	
	Of gentulnes in chivalrye,	
	Ne of ladyes so great rowtes,	
2060	Ne so besene, as all abowghtes	*fine-looking*
	They were there, I certefye	
	You and my lyffe, witheout lye.	*on my life*
	And the feast helde was in tentes —	
	As to tell you myne intent is —	
2065	In a rome, a large playne,	*great open space*
	Under a wood in a champayne,	*Close by; open meadow*
	Betwene a ryver and a well,	*spring*
	Where never had abby ne sell	*monastic cell*
	Ben, ne kyrke, house, ne village,	

---

[1] *Now gave command that all exert themselves*

[2] *And caused these things to be made known to everyone*

2070	In tyme of any manes age.	*man's*
	And dured thre monethes the feast	*lasted*
	In one estate, and never ceste	*In unvarying splendor; ceased*
	From earlye the ryssinge of the sune	
	Till the daye spent was and rune,	
2075	In justinge, dauncesinge, and lustines,	
	And all that sowned to gentulnes. [1]	

	And, as me thowght, the second morrowe,	
	When endid was all old sorrowe	
	And in suertye everye wight	*in the security [of wedlock]*
2080	Had withe his ladye slepte a nyght,	
	The prince, the quene, and all the feast,	
	Unto my ladye made request,	
	And her besowght and ofte prayed	
	To mewardes to be well paied,	*Towards me; pleased*
2085	And consyther myne olde trothe,	*consider*
	And one my paines to have rothe,	
	And me accepte to her service	
	In suche forme, and in suche wyse,	
	That we bothe myght be as one:	
2090	Thus prayde the quene and everyechone.	
	And for ther shuld be no 'naye,'	
	They stinte justinge all a daye	*stopped*
	To praye my ladye and requier	
	Be content and owt of feare,	*[Her to] be*
2095	And withe good hart make frindlye chere,	
	And sayd yt was an happye yere.	
	At wiche she smyled and sayd, 'Iwis,	
	I trow well he my servante is,	
	And wold my welfare, as I trist.	*[he] desires; trust*
2100	So wold I his, and wolde he wist	*wished he knew*
	How, and I knew his trothe	*How, if I knew*
	Contynewe wold witheout slouthe	
	And be suche as ye here reporte,	
	Restraynynge bothe corrage and sport,	*free and wanton spirit*
2105	And couthe consent at youre request	

---

[1] *And everything that was in accordance with gentilesse*

	To be named of your feast,	*named [as one]*
	And do so after your usaunce	
	In obeyinge your pleasaunce;	
	At your request, thus I concent	
2110	To please you in youre entent,	*in what you purpose*
	As eke the soveraynge above	
	Comaunded hathe me for to love	
	And before other him prefarre,	
	Agaynst wiche prince may be no warr,	
2115	For his power over all reynegthe,	
	That other wold for nowght him paynethe.[1]	
	And sythe his will and yours is one,	
	Contrarye in me shal be none.'	

	Tho, as me thowght, the promesse	
2120	Of marriage before the messe	*mass*
	Desyred was — of every wight —	
	To be made the same nyght,	
	To put awaye all maner dowbtes	
	Of everye wyght there abowtes;	
2125	And so was do. And one the morrow,	*done; on*
	When every thowght and every sorrowe	
	Dislodged was owt of myne harte,	
	Withe everye wo and every smarte,	
	Unto a tente the prince and princesse,	
2130	Me thowght, me browght and my misteris,	*mistress*
	And sayd we were at full age	
	Ther to conclud our marriage,	
	Withe ladyes, knyghtes, and squiers,	
	And a great hoost of mynistres	*minstrels*
2135	Withe instrumentes and soundes diverse,	
	That longe were here you to reherse.	
	Wiche tente was churche perochiall,	*And this tent; parochial*
	Ordeyned it was in especiall	
	For the feast and for the sacre,	*sacred ceremony*
2140	Where arshebyshope and archedyaker	*archdeacon*
	Sunge full owt the service,	*with full voice*

---

[1] *Anyone who desires aught else is exerting himself for nothing*

	After the custome and the gyse	*fashion*
	And the churches ordinaunce;	
	And after that, to dyne and daunce	
2145	Browght were we unto diverse pleyes.	*entertainments*
	And, for oure spede, eache wihte prayse,	*person prays*
	And merrye was most and lest;	
	And sayd amended was the feast	
	And where right glad, ladye and lord,	*were*
2150	Of the marriage and th' accorde,	
	And wished us hartes pleasaunce,	
	Joye, hele, and continuaunce;	
	And to the minsterelles made request	
	That in increasynge of the feast	*to add to the pleasure of*
2155	Thay wold tuche ther cordes,	*strings*
	And withe some newe joyeux accordes	*harmonies*
	Meve the pepull to gladnes,	
	And prayden of all gentulnes	
	Eche to paine him, for the daye,	
2160	To shew his conninge and his pleye.	*skill in playing*

	Tho begane sowndes marvelus,	
	And intuned withe accordes joyeux,	*all in tune; harmonies*
	Rounde abowte all the tentes,	
	Withe thousanndes of instrumentes,	
2165	That everye wyght to daunce him pained,	
	To be merye was none that fayned;	
	Wiche so me trowbeled in my slepe,	
	That from my bed forthe I lepe,	*leapt*
	Weninge to be at the feast.	*Thinking [I was]*
2170	But when I wocke, all was ceaste.	*woke; ceased*
	For ther was ladye, ne creature,	
	Save one the walles old portrature	
	Of horsemen, hawkes, and houndes,	
	And hurte deare full of woundes,	
2175	Some lyke bytton, some hurtte with shott,	*as if bitten*
	And, as my dreme, semed that was not.[1]	

---

[1] *And, like my dream, it was all illusion*

127

And when I wocke and knew the trothe,
Had ye sene, of verye rothe
I trow ye wold have wepte a wecke;   *week*
2180   For never man yet halfe so sike
Escaped, I wene, withe the lyfe;   *with his life*
And was for faute that sword ne knyfe   *only for want*
I find myght, my lyve t' abrege,   *shorten*
Ne thinge that carved, ne had edge,
2185   Wherewithe I might my wofull peines
Have voyd withe bledinge of my veynes.   *ended*
Lo, here my blysse! Lo, here my payne!
Whiche to my lady I complayne,
And grace and mercy her requier,
2190   To ende my wo and besy fere,   *urgent anxiety*
And me accepte to her service
After her pleasaunce, in suche wise
That of my dreame the substaunce
Might turne once to cognisaunce, [1]
2195   And cognisaunce to very preve,   *absolute proof*
By full concent and good leave;
Or else, witheowten more, I pray
That this night, or yt be daye,
I mote unto my dreame retorne,   *may*
2200   And slepinge so, forthe ay sojorne
Abowte the Ile of pleasaunce,
Under my ladyes obeysaunce,   *rule*
In her service, and in suche wyse
As yt please her may to devise,
2205   And grace once to be accepte,   *[be granted] grace one day*
Like as I dremed when I slepte,
And duer a thousannd yeres and tene   *And [may I] endure; ten*
In His good grace. Amen. Amen.

EXPLICIT

---

[1] *Might turn some day to acknowledgment of fact*

Fayrest of fayer and goodleste on lyve,   *alive*
2210   All my secre to you I playne and shreve,   *lament and confess*
Requiringe grace, and of all my complainte
To be heled, or martered as a saynt;
For by my trothe I swere, and by this booke,
Ye may bothe hele and slaye me with a looke.

2215   Go forthe myn owne trew harte innocent,
And withe humblenesse do thine observaunce,
And to thi lady on thi knes present
Thi service new, and thinke how great plesaunce
Hit is to lyve under the obeysaunce   *sway*
2220   Of her, that may withe her lookes softe
Geve the blisse that thou desyers ofte.

Be diligent, awacke, obye, and dread,
And not to wilde of thi countenaunce,   *too*
But meke and glade, and thi nature fead   *nurture*
2225   To do eche thinge that may her pleasaunce.   *may [give] her*
When you shall slepe, have ay in remembraunce
The image of her whiche may withe lookes softe
Geve the blysse that thou desyers ofte.

And yf so be that thou her name finde,
2230   Writton in booke or else uppon wall,
Looke that thou do as servaunte trew and kynde
Thine obeysaunce, as she were ther witheall.   *obedient service*
Fayninge in love is breadinge of a fall   *original source of*
From the grace of her, whose lookes softe
2235   May geve the blisse that thou desyers ofte.

FINIS

[Added in a different hand]

Ye that this balade rede shall,
I pray you kepe you from the fall.

FINIS QUOD CHAUCER

Notes

1-6 The reclothing of the bare earth after winter in the mantle of Flora is a common motif in the spring-opening (for which see *FL* 1-14).

10-14 It was not unusual for a beautiful lady to be described as a masterpiece of Nature's handiwork (e.g., Chaucer's description of Virginia in The Physician's Tale, VI.9), but God the Creator is not so commonly invoked. The daringly suggestive use of religious imagery and allusion in relation to sexual love, which was fraught with irony and a sense of dangerous transgression in the best of the earlier poetry (e.g., *Troilus and Criseyde*), seems to have declined here to a more straightforward conceit.

20 *huntinge* is often associated with love-visions, partly because of the opportunities it gives for allusion to the hounds of desire, wounded h(e)arts, etc. See 2172-76.

22 *halfe on slepe*. Medieval authorities on dreams thought that the moments between waking and slumber produced particularly vivid dreams.

25-31 *what I dreamed*. The idea that the dream was as real as real experience (see also 43-50) and occurred in a state not much different from waking is familiar in the discussions of dreams which frequently appear in dreampoems (e.g., Chaucer's *The House of Fame* 1-58).

35 *axes and heale*: one of the traditional paradoxes (cf. fire and freezing cold) of the oxymoron of love.

43-50 The assertion that the dream has an oracular significance, beyond that of a mere dream, echoes similar assertions in the *Romaunt of the Rose* 11-20, and of course Chauntecler's discussion of dreams in The Nun's Priest's Tale.

54-55   There is a degree of sophisticated self-consciousness in the dreamer's recognition of the appropriateness of what he is doing to what is conventionally done.

60   *slepe wrightter*: 'sleep-writer' is rather charming, but it sounds modern, and one suspects that *slepe* is a form of or a mistake for *slepye* (the reading of the other manuscript of *IL*). The sense would not be 'somnolent' but 'sleeping' (note the contrast with *on that wakinge is* in line 62) or 'having to do with sleep.'

63-70   The apology for the writer's *boysteousnes* is a conventional 'modesty-topos,' employed with especial frequency by Lydgate; but it is unusual for the writer to suggest that he be excused because he is relating a dream, or that the reader should take no notice of his lack of skill (usually the reader is asked to emend or correct where he sees fit). As often, the tone suggests not ignorance of the conventions but a carelessly sophisticated mock-naiveté somewhat reminiscent of Chaucer.

71   *an ylle*. Courtly love-visions are occasionally located on islands, but paradisal islands inhabited only by women are particularly characteristic of the Celtic tradition of the 'maidenland' (see Daly, ed. *IL*, pp. 50-54).

72   *of glasse*. There are temples of glass in Chaucer's *The House of Fame* and of course in Lydgate's *Temple of Glass*, as also in Stephen Hawes's *Pastime of Pleasure*, which has many palaces like this one.

73   *closed*. Both the traditional garden of love (e.g., *Romaunt of the Rose* 138) and the allegorical garden of female chastity and beauty (as here, and in the *hortus conclusus* of the Song of Songs) are conventionally enclosed by a wall.

77   *fannes*: decorative weathervanes are a feature of late fifteenth-century palaces, both real and feigned (see *AL* 161). Musical weathervanes of solid gold, in thousands, with pairs of artificial singing birds set upon them, are a touch of fantasy (though they recall the hydraulically-operated birds that adorned the emperor's throne in Byzantium).

81-84   The flowers carved on the towers, like other features of the palace, suggest both beauty and a degree of unnaturalness in the artifice, as may be appropriate to the allegory.

90   *all and womanhed*: an unusual phrase, but cf. 'all and some' (as in line 208).

116   *she nas younge.* There seems no particular reason in the allegory why the lady should be elderly; indeed she ought not to be, given the power of the three apples. There may be some allusion to real life, whether casual and general (she is a kind of governess to this troupe of girls) or covert and specific.

176   *Benedicite.* See *AL* 148n.

194-202 *Fortunes purveaunce.* The narrator hints here at a complaint against Fortune, for her fickle treatment of him, despite his truth (197), presumably in love. It is conventional, and has to do with what follows, but in relation to his arrival on the isle it is a little uncomplimentary to the ladies.

298   *all that vironed is withe see*: i.e., the whole world, which was represented in maps as a single land-mass surrounded by ocean, and not, of course, the Isle of the poem.

306   *in one clothinge*: may suggest a livery, or form of dress worn by all the members of a particular household.

331   *on a roche.* The location of the 'heavenly hermitage' is rather like the dwelling place of Fortune in the *Romaunt of the Rose* (5921), a rocky island way out in the sea.

340   *apples three.* The golden apples of the Hesperides, also the object of a quest, are the best known otherworldly apples, but the closest parallels are in Irish literature, from which Daly (ed. *IL*, p. 294) cites the story of the land of Emne, famous for its apple trees, a land of women where all live free from grief, sickness, and death.

346 *nexst.* It is hard to see how the apple that is highest on the tree can be nearest (*nexst*) to the observer.

407 *leche*: a term usually thought appropriate to the relationship of a lady to her lover.

418 *our brother frinde*: 'our brother's friend.' This can only refer to the dreamer, but the queen is not supposed to know at this point of the existence and presence of the dreamer.

436 *a world of ladyes.* Cf. *FL* 137.

463 *playe.* The playfulness is of course related to the delicacy of the commission and the entrusting of it to *the aged lady*, who will not be so much affected by its delicacy. This aged lady understands the implication, as we see by her smile (481).

520 *sowninge.* The swooning is a good sign: it indicates that the knight is truly noble and gentle at heart. It is not a sign of unmanly weakness, as modern readers often assume, for example in relation to Troilus's swoon (*Troilus*, III.1092).

561-62 The queen's anxiety is reminiscent of that of Criseyde in *Troilus*, II.459-62, and witnesses to a similar struggle between the restraint demanded by an honorable reputation and the fear that excessively severe behavior may do even more harm to that reputation. It is a classic little cameo of internal sentimental debate.

588 The knight's speechlessness is like that of Troilus, when Criseyde comes to his bedside. Troilus, similarly, for all his prepared speeches, can manage only the reiterated cry for mercy (*Troilus*, III.98).

613 *To thi dishonour.* It will be to death's dishonor if he dies since death prides himself on opposing man's will to live.

619 His *cowardice* must be his unmanly behavior in trying to seize the queen by force (line 384).

641   Cf. *Troilus,* II.541: 'And gan to motre, I noot what. . . .'

669-81 The queen's sympathy and care for the knight is richly balanced against her refusal to make any personal commitment to him other than that of womanly compassion.

708   *Aftercastelles*: refers to the elaborate wooden structures built high above deck, in this case aft (cf. forecastle), in ships of the late Middle Ages.

711   *toppes*: railed platforms at the head of a mast.

714   *Smale burdes.* The real birds that accompany Love's navy make a nice allegorical contrast with the artificial singing-birds that decorate the island-fortress of the ladies (line 78).

739   *good langauge.* In the past, pleasant noncommittal words have been enough to keep prospective suitors at bay, as we saw with the queen and the knight (569-82, 644-58).

751   *walles of glasse* are an insubstantial defense against the entry of love.

781-91 The portrayal of the God of Love, and especially of his fierce power to wound the heart, owes much to the *Roman de la Rose* (see *Romaunt,* especially 1723-29).

794   Note the use of the second person singular pronoun in this speech, implying the close relationship of lord to servant. Elsewhere in the poem the more polite and formal second person plural is used, except in the knight's apostrophe to death (607-17), where the singular is suggestive of contempt, and the poet's address to his heart (2215-35), where it conveys intimacy.

816   *his owne lodginge.* Pity's natural dwelling-place is the lady's heart, as medieval poets reiterate constantly.

834   *by requeste.* There is an explicit contrast between what the God of Love commands of others and what he requests of the poet's lady.

838   *consentes*: the Northern dialectal form of the imperative plural.

866 *that mightye saynte.* The God of Love is called *Seynt Amour* in the *Romaunt of the Rose* 6781. The poet of *IL* does not make much of these religious associations (see 10n); he treats the God of Love more as a feudal lord than as a divinity.

888 *So thowght I.* This introduces the alternative to the first, more cheerful thought of line 883 (*as I thowght*).

902 *the yere of grace.* A play on words: the 'year of grace' is when he will win his lady's favor; it is also a form of reference to the year in the Christian era, *anno gratiae* (cf. *anno domini*).

920 *A byll.* For a discussion of such bills and their presence in poems of this kind see *AL* 325n.

943 *his sleve.* The capacious hanging sleeves that were part of the fashionable costume of the time must have been very handy on occasions such as these.

952 *flowers.* The wearing of flowers, especially chaplets of flowers, was commonly associated with the service of love. See *Romaunt of the Rose* 887-917. *FL* has some variations on the convention.

973 *old romansys.* The reading of romances is an aristocratic pastime frequently alluded to in love-poetry. So Pandarus composes himself 'as for to looke upon an old romaunce' (*Troilus,* III.980), and the narrator of *The Book of the Duchess* bids one pass him a book, a 'romaunce,' to 'drive the night away' (47-49). See here, 977.

979 *the spere*: that one of the concentric spheres surrounding the earth in which the sun was fixed and which caused the sun's (apparent) movement.

990 *up in the eyer*: presumably upon some raised platform or scaffold, such as would be erected for a tournament, as in The Knight's Tale, I.2533.

1097 The *statutes* of the God of Love are frequently alluded to, as in the classic text, the *De Arte Honeste Amandi* of the late twelfth-century Andreas Capellanus, or in the *Romaunt of the Rose* 2175 ff., where Love gives his 'comaundementis' (2137), or, more playfully, in the early sixteenth-century

135

Chaucerian pastiche, *The Court of Love*. There are some examples of love's commandments in the present poet's Envoy to his heart (2215-35).

1150   *as wood man*. These lines (1150-66) allegorize the stifling feeling of panic that the lover experiences at the fear of losing his lady.

1153-54   *wave: overthrowghe*. The original rhyme must have been *wawe: overthrawe*, the latter form one of several indications of the northern or north midland provenance of the original poet.

1167   *my testament*. Troilus likewise advises Pandarus of his funeral arrangements when he fears he has lost his lady (*Troilus*, V.295-315).

1195   *of her apples*. This is the second time the lady has used one of her apples (cf. 401) for purposes of resuscitation. *in my sleve*. See 943n.

1209   *He that all joyes*, etc. Such references are commonly ambiguous in love-poetry, but here the allusion is clearly (see line 1216) to the Creator, not the God of Love.

1242   *on consyte*. The phrase is problematic, and the interpretation offered here, taking *consyte* as a form of *conceit* (opinion, view), is one of a number of possibilities.

1301-49   The waking from the dream in the smoke-filled room, the change of location and return to the dream are an unusual and effective device for renewing the impetus and interest of the narrative. Only *Piers Plowman* comes to mind as a poem which makes similar use of connected but separate dreams (eight in number, in that case).

1324   *a chaumbre painte*. Rooms decorated with narrative wall-paintings are a favorite feature of love-vision poems. See *AL* 456n. For their significance here, see 2172-74.

1377   In speaking of the *barge* of *manes thowght*, the poet is making an explicit allegory of one of the most universal of metaphors for the inner life of thought and imagination: the opening lines of Dante's *Purgatorio*, or of

Book II of *Troilus*, are famous examples, as is the Petrarch sonnet adapted by Sir Thomas Wyatt in 'My galley charged with forgetfulness.'

1379-80 The allegorical suggestion here is that the queen is active in the knight's inner life.

1381 *nether mast ne rother*. Rudderless boats are common in folk-literature, and are especially associated with journeys to the otherworld in Celtic tradition.

1505-06 Failure to keep to the letter a promise to return to one's lady by a set date was a mortal sin in love-romance. Chrétien's Yvain spends the greater part of the romance of *Yvain* regretting and expiating just such a failure. Here the knight could hardly complain that the matter was not made quite clear (1361-72). More generally, plots that rely on the consequences of the violation of a prohibition are very common in folk-literature.

1555-65 The boat's miraculous capacity: Daly (ed. *IL*, pp. 313-14) compares the story of the shirt of Joseph of Arimathaea in Robert de Boron's *History of the Holy Grail* (translated into English in the early fifteenth century by Herry Lovelich), in which 150 sail to Britain.

1571 *sayd was the crede*. It was customary to offer prayers for a safe voyage before setting out.

1674 *an open weye*. The phrase has a strong suggestion of female promiscuity, explicit in the proverb alluded to in *Piers Plowman*, C.III.167, where the maiden Meed is 'As comyn as the cartway to knaves and to alle.'

1679-80 *thrise . . . twise*. What looks like an arcane bit of administrative detail is certainly due, like much in the poem, to nothing more than the exigencies of rhyme.

1799 *nonnes . . . blacke*: an abbey of Benedictine nuns.

1864 *An erb*. The most striking analogue for this episode is in the *Lai d'Eliduc* of Marie de France (twelfth century), where a dead weasel is restored to life by its mate with a magic plant. The plant is then used to revive the maiden Guillardon. The motif of an animal reviving its companion or mate with a magic herb is widespread, especially in Celtic tradition, as in Marie. The animals are most often snakes.

1917   *of ther lord.* Presumably the sight of the lady brings to the minds of the assembled company (mostly the knight's retinue, since the ladies are all dead or dying) the sad fate of their lord.

1923   *Thre.* The bird sang *thre songes* (1832), and so there are three *greynes*. The scene is reminiscent of The Prioress's Tale, where the *greyn* on his tongue keeps the child miraculously alive after his throat has been cut.

1939   The queen takes over the role of the abbess, and thus acts out literally her metaphorical role as *leche* to the knight.

1955   *of ladyes . . . a rowte.* The *two partes* (two thirds) of the ladies who died (1649-52) are now restored to life.

1974   *parlament.* For the difference between an *assemble* (1971) and a *parlament,* see *AL* 720n.

2050   *Seynt John to borowe*: a formulaic prayer to ward off bad luck, as at leavetaking or the making of promises. Cf. The Squire's Tale, V.596.

2063   *in tentes.* Great outdoor feasts were commonly held in tented pavilions.

2111   *the soveraynge above*: i.e., the God of Love, whose commands to the lady were outlined in 803-77.

2113   *him*: i.e., the dreamer.

2137   *churche perochiall.* The dreamer's care to affirm that he was married, in his dream, in a tent which was actually his own proper parish church, is of a piece, in its wry pragmatism, with the frustration he accepts in being the only one who does not get to sleep with his lady.

2167   The moment of sudden waking is often carefully prepared for in dream-poems (see *AL* 726n), and the noise of singing and music is a frequent motif in such awakenings, as in Lydgate's *Temple of Glass.* Here the noise of music at the wedding disturbs the dreamer's sleep, and it is natural that he should wish to be present in person at his own marriage feast.

2172 For the appropriateness of such hunting-scenes to the lover's situation, see 20n.

2187 *Lo, here . . . Lo, here*: echoes *Troilus*, V.1849-55.

2194-95 *cognisaunce . . . preve.* There is a legal conceit here, alluding to the difference between acknowledgement of an alleged fact and the evidential demonstration of its truth.

2208 *His.* Other texts and editors have *her*, which makes better sense, but is clearly not a harder reading, and thus may be one that a scribe may well have preferred. The sense of 'His' would be rather audacious: that dwelling in his lady's grace would be to dwell also in God's.

2209-35 For his Envoy, or epilogue, the poet turns from the octosyllabic couplet to the pentameter, as do Gower and Lydgate on similar occasions. The first stanza, addressed to the lady, is a sixain in couplets, and is independent in both dramatic and metrical form from the rest. The other three stanzas are in rhyme royal, with repeated last line as in the true envoy, and are addressed to his heart. There is no reason to think that lines 2209-35 were not part of the original poem of *IL*.

2215 *Go forthe.* The apostrophe in such epilogues is usually to the poet's *litel bok* (as in *Troilus*, V.1786). The poet here works a rather neat variation on the convention, apostrophizing his heart and swearing upon his book as if it were a bible.

2226 *you.* The appropriateness of the use of the second person singular in the poet's address to his heart has been noted (794n). It is hard to tell whether this anomalous *you* is the poet's or the scribe's slip.

2233-35 The religious allusion is nicely pointed: falsehood leads to a fall from grace which loses the promise of bliss.

2237 *fall*: i.e., the fall from grace mentioned in 2233. These last two lines, though they appear in all three early texts, are very probably a spurious addition. The hand that adds the final hopeful attribution (only in the Longleat manuscript) has also crossed out the earlier *Finis*.

Bibliography

Bibliographies

Rossell Hope Robbins. 'The Chaucerian Apocrypha,' in *A Manual of the Writings in Middle English*, ed. Albert E. Hartung (New Haven: Connecticut Academy of Arts and Sciences, 1974). Volume IV, chapter XI, pp. 1094-97, 1302-05.

Russell A. Peck. *Chaucer's Romaunt of the Rose and Boece, Treatise on the Astrolabe, Equatorie of the Planetis, Lost Works and Chaucerian Apocrypha: An Annotated Bibliography 1900-1985* (Toronto: University of Toronto Press, 1988). Pp. 308-09, 317-21, 325-26.

Editions

W. W. Skeat, ed. *Chaucerian and Other Pieces*. Volume VII of *The Works of Chaucer* (Oxford: Oxford University Press, 1897). Editions of *FL* and *AL*.

D. A. Pearsall, ed. *The Floure and the Leafe and The Assembly of Ladies*. Nelson's Medieval and Renaissance Library (London and Edinburgh: Thomas Nelson, 1962; reprinted Manchester University Press, Old and Middle English Texts Series, 1980).

Anthony Jenkins, ed. *The Isle of Ladies or the Ile of Pleasaunce*. Garland Medieval Texts, Number 2 (New York and London: Garland Publishing, 1980).

Vincent Daly, ed. *A Critical Edition of The Isle of Ladies*. The Renaissance Imagination: Important Literary and Theatrical Texts from the Late Middle Ages through the Seventeenth Century. Volume 28 (New York and London: Garland Publishing, 1987). Typescript of Harvard University Ph.D. thesis, 1977.

Bibliography

Critical Studies

G. L. Marsh, 'Sources and Analogues of *The Flower and the Leaf,*' *Modern Philology*, 4 (1906-07), 121-68, 281-328.

Eleanor Prescott Hammond, ed. *English Verse between Chaucer and Surrey* (Durham, North Carolina: Duke University Press, 1927). Texts and excellent commentary. Invaluable background.

C. S. Lewis. *The Allegory of Love* (Oxford: Oxford University Press, 1936). See especially pp. 247-49.

Ethel Seaton. *Sir Richard Roos: Lancastrian Poet* (London: Rupert Hart-Davis, 1961). Valuable literary and social background, especially in chapters I and II; the authorship attributions (all three poems are ascribed to Roos) are not to be taken seriously.

John Stevens. *Music and Poetry in the Early Tudor Court* (London: Methuen, 1961). See especially chapter 9, 'The Game of Love,' pp. 154-202 (*AL*, 179-80; *FL*, 180-02).

Derek Pearsall, 'The English Chaucerians,' in D. S. Brewer, ed., *Chaucer and Chaucerians: Critical Studies in Middle English Literature* (London and Edinburgh: Thomas Nelson, 1966), pp. 201-39 (especially 225-30).

David V. Harrington, 'The Function of Allegory in *The Flower and the Leaf,*' *Neuphilologische Mitteilungen*, 71 (1970), 244-53.

John Stephens, 'The Questioning of Love in the *Assembly of Ladies,*' *Review of English Studies*, n.s. 24 (1973), 129-40.

Richard Firth Green. *Poets and Princepleasers: Literature and the English Court in the Late Middle Ages* (Toronto: University of Toronto Press, 1980). See especially chapter 4, 'The Court of Cupid.'

Ann McMillan, '"Fayre Sisters Al': *The Flower and the Leafe* and *The Assembly of Ladies,*' *Tulsa Studies in Women's Literature*, 1 (1982), 27-42.

Alexandra A. T. Barratt, '"The Flower and the Leaf' and 'The Assembly of Ladies': Is There a (Sexual) Difference?' *Philological Quarterly*, 66 (1987), 1-24.

Glossary

afor(n)e *before*

after, aftir *after, according to*

agayne, ageyne *see* **ayen, ayenst**

al, alle *all*

anon(e), annon(e) *soon, straightway*

appaide, appayed *pleased*

avise, advise *consider, advise, look at, look around*

avised (past participle) *determined, resolved, advised (as in well-advised)*

ayen, agayne(s), ageyne(s) *again, in reply*

ayenst, agayne(s), ageyne(s) *against, to meet*

bare, bere *bore*

be *by*

be(n) (present plural) *are*

be(n) (past participle) *been*

ben(e) (infinitive) *be*

bien *be, are*

by and by *in succession, one by one, point by point*

cace, case *case, matter, affair*

can(e), con(e) *is able to, can;* also as auxiliary for preterite (*=did*)

cauled (past participle) *called*

certayne, certeyne, sertayne, for certayne, in certayne *certainly, truly, indeed*

chekes *cheeks*

chere *face, demeanor, manner, expression, disposition*

com(en) *came*

con *see* **can**

coninge, connynge *skill, knowledge, courtesy*

con(n)inglye *wisely, politely, skillfully*

coud *could*

couth(e), cothe, cuthe *could, knew, knew how to*

cowde, culd *could*

deale, dele, dell, every dele *part, bit, portion, every bit, thoroughly*

devise *describe, imagine, conceive, relate*

dewer *see* **duer**

do(n) (past participle) *done*

doubt(e), dout(e), dowbt(e), dowt *fear, doubt*

duer, dure, dewer *endure, last, survive*

dyvers *various, different*

ech(e) *each*

ech(e)on(e) *each one, every one*

eke, eak *also*

ensure *assure*

entent(e) *purpose, mind*

even *right, immediately*

everich(on), everichone, everychone *every one, each one*

eyne *eyes*

143

faine, fayne *glad, gladly*
faute, feaute *fault, defect*
fayer *fair*
fer(re) *far, afar*
fere, feere, feare *fellowship, company*
in fere *in company, together, as well, completely*
feyre *fair*
fil *fell*
flour(es) *flower(s)*
fore *for*
fro *from*
ful(l) *very*
furth *forth, further, onward*

gan *began* (but shading off to *did*)
gefe, geve *give*
go *gone*
grete *great, greatly*

hard, herd *heard*
heale, hele *health, happiness, well-being*
hede *head*
hem *them*
her, hir *their*
herber *arbor*
here *hear*
hether *hither*
hew *hue*
hie, hye *high*
hight *is called*
hir *her; their*
hol(e), holl(e) *whole, entire;* **hole the** *all of the*
hole, holl, holly(e) *wholly, entirely*
hond *hand*
horse *horse, horses, horse's*

hye *high*

iwis *indeed*

joyeuse, joyeux, joyoux *joyful*

knene *knees*
know(e) *known*

late *let*
laurer, laurey *laurel*
leche *physician (leech); see notes to IL 407 and 1939*
leke, liche, lyke *like, alike, as if*
lenger *longer*
lest(e) *least*
list *wished*
list (him) *it pleased (him)*
lite(l) *little*
lusty(e) *happy, pleasant, pleasure-loving, lively, vigorous*
lyves *alive, living*

maner(e) *kind (of), way*
matere, matier(e) *matter, affair, business, suit, petition*
mede *meadow*
moche *much*
mo(o) *more, others*
mot(e) *must*
myddes *midst*

nat *not*
ne *not, nor*
nede, nead(e) *need, of necessity*
nie, nye *nigh, nearly*
nist, nyst *did not know*

o, oo, oon *one, a single, the same*
obessiaunce, obeysaunce *obedience, submission, sway, rule*
ones *once*
or *ere, before*
ordinaunce *command, decree*

paide, paied, payed *pleased, contented, satisfied*
passyng *very, extremely*
petye *pity*
playe, pleye *speak or act playfully, amuse oneself*
prayed *invited*
pres, presse *crowd, throng*
purfil, purfyll *embroidered or furred hem of garment*

quod *said*

rede *read, advise*
reherce, reherse *recount, tell (of), repeat*
reme *realm*
right *entirely, very, very much*
rothe, routhe, rowth *pity*
route, rowte *company*

sad(d) *steadfast, serious, sober*
san(n)de *see* **sonde**
se *see*
se, see, sie (past tense) *saw*
sene (infinitive) *see*
sertayne *see* **certayne**
sewe, sue *sue, make petition, present (a petition)*
seyne (past participle) *seen*
shul *shall*

sie (past tense) *saw*
silf *self*
sith(e), sythe *since*
sonde, sannde *beach*
song (past tense) *sang*
soth *true, truth*
soth(e)ly, soothly *truly, indeed*
space *while*
sute *suit, matching kind*

than *then*
that *what, whatever, that which*
the *thee*
then *than*
ther(e) *their*
theyr *there*
tho *then*
tho *those*
thorow, thurgh *through, throughout, thorough(ly)*
thought (in me thought) *it seemed to me, I thought*
til *to*
to *too*
to *till, until*
togider, togyder, togydre *together*
travayle, travell *labor, hard work*
trow(e) *believe*

uncoth(e) *strange, unfamiliar, marvellous, curious*
un(n)ethe *hardly, scarcely*
until *unto, to*

veluet *velvet*
very, verray *very, true, genuine, absolute*
viage, vioage *journey*

ware *aware*

ware, were *wore*

wele *well*

wele, welle *happiness, well-being*

wene (past tense **wened, wend**) *think, imagine, suppose*

were *wore*

wete(n) *know*

wex *grew, became*

whan *when*

what *whatever*

wheche, wiche *which*

wight *person, creature, man, one*

wise, wyse *manner, way, kind, kinds (of)*

wit(e) *know*

wol(l) *will, want (to)*

wold *would, wished, wanted to*

wonder (adverb) *wonderfully, very, extremely*

word(e) *motto*

wot(e), wotte *know, knows*

wox(e) *grew, became*

wyt *know*

y *I*

ya(a)te *gate*

yave *gave*

yche *each*

yede(n) *went*

yef *if*

yeve *give(n)*

yis *yes*

yit *yet*

yle, ylle *isle*

Volumes in the Middle English Texts Series

The Floure and the Leafe, The Assemblie of Ladies, and *The Isle of Ladies*, ed. Derek Pearsall (1990)

Three Middle English Charlemagne Romances, ed. Alan Lupack (1990)

Six Ecclesiastical Satires, ed. James M. Dean (1991)

Heroic Women from the Old Testament in Middle English Verse, ed. Russell A. Peck (1991)

The Canterbury Tales: Fifteenth-Century Continuations and Additions, ed. John M. Bowers (1992)

Gavin Douglas, *The Palis of Honoure*, ed. David J. Parkinson (1992)

Wynnere and Wastoure and *The Parlement of the Thre Ages*, ed. Warren Ginsberg (1992)

The Shewings of Julian of Norwich, ed. Georgia Ronan Crampton (1994)

King Arthur's Death: The Stanzaic Morte Arthur and *The Alliterative Morte Arthure*, ed. Larry D. Benson and Edward E. Foster (1994)

Lancelot of the Laik and *Sir Tristrem*, ed. Alan Lupack (1994)

Sir Gawain: Eleven Romances and Tales, ed. Thomas Hahn (1995)

The Middle English Breton Lays, ed. Anne Laskaya and Eve Salisbury (1995)

Sir Perceval of Galles and *Ywain and Gawain*, ed. Mary Flowers Braswell (1995)

Four Middle English Romances: Sir Isumbras, Octavian, Sir Eglamour of Artois, Sir Tryamour, ed. Harriet Hudson (1996)

The Poems of Laurence Minot (1333-1352), ed. Richard H. Osberg (1996)

Medieval English Political Writings, ed. James M. Dean (1996)

The Book of Margery Kempe, ed. Lynn Staley (1996)

The Cloud of Unknowing, ed. Patrick Gallacher (1997)

Amis and Amiloun, Robert of Ciseyle, and Sir Amadace, ed. Edward E. Foster (1997)

Robin Hood and Other Outlaw Tales, ed. Stephen Knight and Thomas Ohlgren (1997)

To order please contact:

MEDIEVAL INSTITUTE PUBLICATIONS
Western Michigan University
Kalamazoo, MI 49008-3801
Phone (616) 387-8755
FAX (616) 387-8750